STEVE SUCCESS ADEBAYO ADEWOLE

SMART

Produced by Wisdom House Publications

Printed by
Bela Printing Consult

All rights reserved

First Edition

Copyright @ 2022 by Steve Success Adebayo Adewole

Printed by
Bela Printing Consult

BELA PUBLICATIONS

DEDICATION

MY QUEEN

I cannot but thank God for the mother of the house, Honour Ibilola Adewole - my beloved wife, confidant, friend, Olori, my Queen - in your eyes I feel I get lost because they are beautiful, you are too much, your passion for the things of God amazes me, your desire to see others grow takes my fancy; I love you very much. Thanks for being a blessing all the way, sweetheart. If I were a cell phone, you would be the charger. You are the epitome of romance, the pinnacle of commitment and the essence of marital bliss. You are not only the mother of our precious children but also the beat of my heart. You are not just the Queen of the family unit but also the woman of my dreams.

You have made my imperfections seem perfect and all my shortcomings appear complete. I don't know how I will ever be able to thank you for everything you have done but I promise, I will never stop trying. I since discovered that I don't need to add sugar in my coffee because your kisses are all the sweetness I need in my life. If you replace L in life with W, you get wife, that is because life isn't worth living without a lovely wife like you. No matter how hard and punishing a day has been, I know I will always be together at the close of the day with the most beautiful woman on the planet earth.

The PK - Emmanuel & Anointed

Emmanuel and Anointed – you are the best compliment that destiny has given us. Your maturity is way beyond your ages. You have a strong admirable personalities beyond your ages. Your focus in life is commendable, children you are truly special; in our lives' horizon, you are the brightest stars. Thanks for being the wonderful children that you are supporting and committed to the work at hand. All parents wish the world for their children but only few children like yourselves give the world to their parents in return.

Thanks for making us realise that we have made an important contribution to the world by given birth to intelligent and noble children like yourselves. We love you both and your love for God gives us joy. Keep the fire burning.

ACKNOWLEDGMENT

I give thanks to the Almighty God, the FATHER, the SON and the HOLY SPIRIT for the enablement to complete this project, SMART, successfully.

Wisdom House Family are super awesome people and there is no way we could have spell Success as a Ministry without your continuous dedication and absolute commitment.

You are absolutely fabulous, fantastic and incredibly great people.

CONTENTS

Introduction

Smart will encourage, motivate, empower and furnish you with wisdom that you need to conduct the affairs of your life. It will place a demand on you not to die with your music still in you; you are required to die empty by fulfilling purpose.

TAKE NOTE #1A

—

Interesting Story

History student Ellie Johnson had been suffering from abdominal pain for months and suspected she had some kind of 'blockage' in her body.

She didn't expect that 'blockage' to be a baby, and only discovered the truth when her child's head emerged.

Ellie, 24, was taking the contraceptive pill and says she didn't have any symptoms apart from tummy pain while unknowingly pregnant.

The then masters student even took three pregnancy tests, which all came back negative.

And two days before giving birth, Ellie's pain prompted her to get an ultrasound – where, again, she claims doctors didn't spot the pregnancy.

Ellie, of Henham, Essex, said: 'I didn't know I was pregnant until I was giving birth.

'I was on the contraceptive pill. I was taking it every day and even through my pregnancy, I was taking it every day.

'I didn't really have any symptoms. I was still having periods every month and didn't have a bump or anything like that.

'The weekend before she was born I flew up to Edinburgh and was out on a pub crawl for two nights for my friend's birthday and then flew back home and was horrifically sick on the plane. I just thought it was because of the weekend.

'Up until she literally dropped out of me, I was going to university four times a week and that was a four-hour round trip every day.I was also travelling to a volunteership one day a week and working two retail jobs, so I didn't really stop.'

The mum-of-one had her first doctor's appointment in September 2018 and saw a gastroenterologist specialist the following month.

Ellie claims she had blood tests where no hormones were detected that indicated that she was expecting.

'The only reason I started going to the doctors was because I had stomach pain, was really uncomfortable and felt like I was putting on weight.

I did a pregnancy test at home and thought "oh, it's negative, it can't be that" and had six doctors say that I wasn't pregnant.

'I went to the doctors and they looked me over, sent me for some blood tests and gave me a pregnancy test while I was there, and it came back negative.

'They thought it was something to do with my digestive system so I was sent to specialists. All of the easy stuff was being ruled out by tests and they thought it was quite serious and that I basically had a blockage somewhere.

'I'd wake up one morning and I'd feel like I'd eaten a full English breakfast, I'd feel full.

'Some mornings the top part of my stomach would be bloated and the next morning I'd wake up and be totally fine, my stomach would be back to normal and I was in my size 10 jeans and off I went.'

On December 20, 2018, Ellie claims she had an ultrasound of her stomach and ribs where she was told that everything appeared normal.

The next day, she went out for dinner and drinks to celebrate her grandmother's birthday, but when she went to bed at around 10pm, she started experiencing horrific stomach and back pain.

After vomiting for four hours, Ellie and her mum called an ambulance and she was taken to A&E.

There, the pain got worse.

'I genuinely thought because of everything, that my intestines were coming out of my bum,' she said.

As she lay on the bed, a nurse and doctors checked Ellie over – then saw her baby's head begin to crown.

'I didn't quite believe it,' said the mum. 'I thought I was hallucinating at that point as well because of the pain and then I had this bundle put next to me and cuddled up with me, and there was a little baby face.'

Little Alicia Johnson was born at 5:40am on December 22, 2018 weighing 6lbs 12oz at around 37 weeks.

The whole ordeal was quite a shock, but Ellie couldn't be happier.

She believes her pregnancy wasn't spotted on the ultrasound because her baby's back was against her spine, and that taking the pill meant pregnancy hormones weren't detected in tests.

Ellie, who now works as an administrator, said: 'Because I was still in that panic mode, my first reaction was "I can't be a mum, I can't do it, please don't."

'I spent 20 minutes alone with her and said "you know what, if my body could have done that, I can do it, it's meant to be" and I just fell in love with her at that point anyway.

'The only way I can describe Alicia is that she's a whirlwind of energy. She's an absolute little fighter, she had nothing wrong with her and we joke that she was pickled through the pregnancy.

'But she is incredible, smart and she started walking when she was 11-months-old. She is just amazing and full of beans.

'I can't imagine my life without her now. It's crazy.'

CHAPTER 1

Don't be in a hurry

Patience is bitter, but its fruit is sweet

Apathy makes excuses while passion finds a way. We are to display the politics of heaven on earth. My beloved in Christ, give it time, God is at work underground hence stop trying to force fruit that is not yet due. You can be intelligent and talented without reaching the top. Until you make up your mind never to quit, you will remain a part of 95% of group of people who never tasted success.

Don't settle for mediocrity; stop mourning and complaining about how life had treated you because the world is not blessed by talkers but by people who are determined to make success out of it.

Pride must die in you or nothing of heaven can live in you. Admit you cannot accomplish your goals by your power or intellect but rather lean on God Apostle Paul said in first Corinthians.

chapter sixteen verse nine – For a great door and effectual is opened unto me, and there are many adversaries. Every opposition is contending for your position hence you must endure against all odds and success will be the outcome.

Pride will cost you everything but leave you with nothing. Spiritual arrogance is dangerous never join the foolish ones to play such a game. Admit you are not adequate in yourself; you need God and we all do. Don't forget that the struggles we endure today will be the 'good old days' we laugh about tomorrow.

Desire is the key to motivation, but it is determination and commitment to an unrelenting pursuit of your goal – a commitment to excellence – that will enable you to attain the success you seek. Resilience requires optimism and strength.

TAKE NOTE #1B

—

Good News: Cats Are Good for Your Health - <u>Edie Jardieu</u>

Scientists studying the human-animal bond have discovered there are health benefits of owning a cat. Yes, even that belittled "black cat" can be good for you!

❖ **Help your cardiovascular system:** Studies at the <u>University of Minnesota</u> determined those who did not own cats were 30-40% more likely to die of cardiovascular disease than cat owners were.

❖ **Help your immune system:** The immune system gets a boost from the feeling you get just by owning a cat. Owning a cat may lead to improved social support, reduced depression, and more laughter, play and exercise

❖ **Avoid allergies and respiratory problems:** Children who are raised around cats (and dogs) develop immunity to allergens at an early age. The incidence of <u>respiratory</u>

<u>problems</u>, including asthma, is reduced in children exposed to cats early in their lives.

* **Lower your blood pressure:** Petting your cat is calming and reduces your blood pressure. Studies at the <u>State University of New York at Buffalo</u> found lower blood pressure in the study subjects who owned pets compared with those who did not

* **Lower your cholesterol and triglycerides:** Diet and exercise go a long way toward reducing cholesterol and triglyceride levels, but owning a cat helps, too. A 2006 <u>Canadian study</u> found owning a cat lowered cholesterol better than even some medications.

* **Reduce your stroke risk:** A University of Minnesota <u>study</u> determined cat ownership can reduce your stroke risk by up to one-third!

* **Heal your bones and muscles:** Cats purr at a frequency between 20-140 Hz, which is known to have <u>therapeutic effects</u>. Bones heal best at 25 Hz and 50 Hz frequencies (and 100 Hz and 200 Hz are also helpful). Soft tissues like muscles, tendons and ligaments heal faster at these frequencies. And infections and swelling are also healed in this frequency range.

❖ **Reduce anxiety and stress:** In today's fast-paced lifestyle, with more work and less socializing, interacting with a pet brings play-time and creativity back into your life. Caring for your cat and cuddling with your cat take your mind off your own worries and reduce your levels of anxiety and stress.

❖ **Improve your mood and depression:** Cats may have the reputation of being solitary, unsocial animals but cat owners know this is not the case. The love and companionship of a cat helps you feel better about life in general and can lift your mood and lessen feelings of depression.

❖ **Reduce Loneliness:** Having a person-cat connection is a form of social interaction. If your group of friends is small, or far away, your cat can help relieve your feelings of loneliness.

❖ **Therapy pets reduce medical expenses:** People who own cats make fewer doctor and hospital visits. When they do visit the hospital, they are discharged earlier. Overall, their medical expenses are reduced.

❖ **Exercise:** Cats don't need as much exercise as dogs, but they still love to play. Make your cat your exercise buddy and help him bat a toy mouse around! Watch your cat and learn how to stretch! Observe how many times your cat stretches – and when he does it – and join in! The "pet effect" can improve your quality of life.

CHAPTER 2

Know You

There are two kinds of people on earth – the TAKERS and the GIVERS. Who are you between the two; *a taker or a giver*? The takers may eat better, but the givers sleep better. It is good to be generous but please don't set yourself on fire to keep others warm. Jesus died for us all but there will be no second cruxification.

We come to realise that successful people are always looking for opportunities to help others. Unsuccessful people are always asking, 'what is in it for me?' However, when givers indulge in a connection, there is a spark; it is alchemy. It is a situation of I water you, you water me, we never drain each other and we just grow together. **In each of us are places where we have never gone. Only by pressing the limits do you ever find them.** Relationship is give and take.

We must be like our heavenly Father – who gives perpetually, and He is never tired of giving. *Are you a giver or a taker only*?

John 3:16 –*For God so greatly loved and dearly prized the world that He [even] gave up His only begotten ([a]unique) Son, so that whoever believes in (trusts in, clings to, relies on) Him shall not perish (come to destruction, be lost) but have eternal (everlasting) life.*

Some main characteristics of givers and takers are:

a) Givers understand reality and human need; takers prefer fantasy and meeting their own needs

b) Givers want to be accountable, responsible citizens but takers really don't want to account to anyone or have many responsibilities

c) Givers realize they may have to wait to get what they want or even do without but takers live by the law of instant gratification

d) Givers look out for their families but takers look out for themselves

e) Givers stick with a marriage when the going gets tough but takers bail out because they are not being fulfilled.

TAKE NOTE #2

—

Health issues

There are two main types of stroke: ischaemic and haemorrhagic. 90 percent of strokes are ischaemic and due to atherosclerosis, the buildup of fatty plaque in the arteries of the brain, which then causes a blockage and deprives the brain of blood.

Can certain foods increase your risk of stroke?

Foods associated with an increased risk of ischaemic stroke include those high in saturated fat, such as meat, particularly processed and unprocessed red meat, and cheese and ultra-processed foods, which are usually high in unhealthy fats, salt and sugar. This type of unhealthy diet increases the risk of developing high blood pressure, high cholesterol, type 2 diabetes and carrying too much weight, key risk factors for developing stroke.

What are the main symptoms of a stroke and the ones some people might miss?

The symptoms depend on which part of the brain is affected, so there are a number of potential symptoms. These include weakness down one side of the body, drooping of one side of the face, loss of vision, difficulty walking or with balance, poor coordination, confusion, loss of speech, loss of sensation on one side of the body.

What should you do if you or someone is having a stroke?

Phone 999 immediately and ask for an ambulance. Express Health

CHAPTER 3

Yearning for God

The key to Christian living is a thirst and hunger for God

The key to Christian living is a thirst and hunger for God. To hunger is to have a strong desire or craving for something. It's that gnawing ache on the inside of you; that sense of need that is not content until it is filled. And hunger for God is the landing strip of the Holy Spirit; it is a signal that God is setting you up for an encounter with Him! For something new is on the horizon—but before you step into your destiny, it's time to catch a fresh revelation of who Jesus is. And deepen your relationship with Him. Hear Him saying, "I want to feast with you. I want to share all that I am with you." - Rev 3:20) There are 3 signs of hunger for God:

You are Dissatisfied with the Status Quo

Hunger for God is often characterized by a feeling of discontent. You sense you are missing something in your relationship with Him. You are no longer satisfied with the degree to which you have known Jesus. You begin to feel restless in that discontent, for the Holy Spirit is drawing you closer to Him.

A Past Encounter with God Stirs Longing in You

You remember a past encounter with God, and it stirs hunger in you. You may find yourself yearning for what is behind—the "good old days" of faith. If you can relate to this, know that what you have tasted before, can be yours again—and more! That longing you have—that hunger—is setting you up for what is to come.

You are Feeling Weak Spiritually Speaking

Awareness of your own spiritual weakness can be painful. But within that trial you're in right now, is an invitation from the Father. For God has a new strength for you, that can only be found in Him. In Him you are able to do all things.

TAKE NOTE #3

—

Dementia warning

Eating at certain times of the day may 'dramatically' harm memory. A substantial amount of research has exposed the deleterious effects of poor meal timing on sleep patterns, weight control and diabetes. Many of the body's biological processes are governed by the body's internal clock - medically known as the circadian rhythm.

Even the slightest disruptions to routine can push our natural cycle out of sync, and the effects this has on the brain are becoming increasingly clear. According to certain studies, eating late at night could offset the body's internal clock and hamper short and long-term memory, setting the stage for dementia.

It's long been known that eating late at night disrupts sleep. In fact, eating just one hour further could significantly reduce sleep-wake cycles. The health body Chronobiology explains this is because people who eat late at night "are more likely to stay up late and not be sleeping at a natural time".

According to the health body, this may reduce synaptic plasticity in the brain, which is the physiological process that allows the organ to store new information.

These effects were confirmed in a study on rodents in 2015, who also showed signs of damage to the liver and adrenal glands when they ate late at night. The researchers established that taking regular meals at the wrong time of the day could have far-reaching effects on both learning and memory.

They discovered that eating at times reversed for sleep led to deficiencies in learning and memory controlled by the hippocampus.

The hippocampal region of the brain enables humans to process and retrieve two types of memory; declarative memory and spatial relationships.

This part of the brain governs both long-term memory and the ability to recognise new objects. Express Health

CHAPTER 4

Winning Mentality

The hallmark of successful people is cheerful optimism, attempting something new, flexible, doing stuff, learning stuff, never lazy about, proactiveness, constantly moving forward are the most fundamental traits of successful people. The Bible says he that does not work must not eat, that is a divine order.

Winners Choose Optimism, Every Time. What is the biggest, most important key to success in life? Attitude! Remember the old saying that "Your attitude determines your altitude?" I'm convinced it's true. Optimism comes naturally and easily to only a few. Perhaps they are wired differently, I don't know. But for the majority of people, optimism is a learned skill, a chosen approach to life. It's a conscious decision to see "the glass as half-full."

Clearly, this is a troubled world and there are lots of problems out there. We can't deny that. But it's also true that, "what we focus on, expands." And, of course, "we become what we think about most of the time." Proverbs 23:7 *says as a man thinketh in his heart so is he.*

If you don't like something, change it. If you can't change it, change your attitude. **Sooner or later, those who win are those who think they can by developing winning mentality.**

Even in tough times, we are rich beyond what you can imagine! And yet the news is almost uniformly bad, bloody and painful most especially with Covid 19 – We worry all day long. People are angry, discouraged, and actively practicing their "victim "approach to life.

Always remind yourself that you are not a VICTIM but a VICTOR through the blood of Jesus Christ which He shed on the CROSS for you and me. High achievers refuse to buy into this negativity! Winners have always looked for the good, emphasized hope, and found opportunity where others see only problems. What do you see? What you see and confess will eventually possess you. Ditch grasshopper mentality today. You are too loaded to fail. Take off garment of defeat and mediocrity.

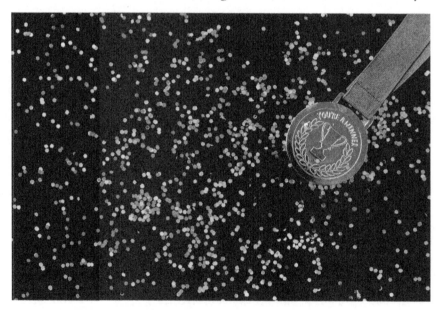

TAKE NOTE #4

—

Pregnancy: Carrots and Kale

Eating carrots during pregnancy makes babies happy and kale turns them to 'tears. Children's hatred of greens - and an apparent love of carrots - start in their mums' wombs, astonishing evidence reveals.Scans of 100 mothers-to-be show foetuses giving more "laughter-face" responses at carrots, but "cry-face" reactions to kale. The findings by scientists at Durham University could now aid research into how human taste and smell receptors develop.They believe what pregnant women could influence their children's taste preferences – and could help form healthy eating habits.It is thought foetuses experience flavour by inhaling and swallowing the womb's amniotic fluid.

Experts recorded reactions soon after the mums took carrot and kale flavour capsules. Postgraduate BeyzaUstun, who led the research, said: "Studies have suggested babies can taste and smell in the womb, but they are based on post-birth outcomes. "Our study is the first to see these reactions prior to birth. We think repeated exposure to flavours before birth could help to establish food preferences post-birth – which could be important when thinking about messaging around healthy eating and the potential for avoiding 'food-fussiness' when weaning.

"It was really amazing to see the unborn babies' reaction and share those moments with their parents." Facial reactions seen in both flavour groups showed exposure to just a small amount of carrot or kale flavour stimulated a response. Research co-author Professor Jackie Blissett, of Aston University, Birmingham, said: "The next step is to examine whether foetuses show less 'negative' responses to these flavours over time, resulting in greater acceptance when babies first taste them outside of the womb." The study appears in the journal Psychological Science Express Health

CHAPTER 5

Tenacity

No other god can compete with the Creator, the BIG Daddy up there!

When the Lord delivered Israel out of Egypt, he executed judgement against all the gods of Egypt. No matter how you feel – get up, dress up, show up, and never ever give up.

Be reminded that every satanic stronghold will have no choice but to bow to stubborn faith and stubborn prayers.

To conquer frustration, you must remain intensely focused on the outcome of your spiritual engagement with the Holy Spirit and not the obstacles such as spiritual apathy. Don't forget that the miraculous is the hallmark of the Bible and the supernatural is the glue which binds the scriptures together.

If you will permit me, let me ask you this question: Are you desperate or determined? Please note that with desperation comes frustration: Frustration bring about anger, irritability, stress, upset, helplessness, resentment, depression and spiral downward; frustration set in when expectation does not match the efforts you put in. Frustration is very destructive hence you must refuse to be frustrated.

But first and foremost, with determination comes purpose; purpose as you might have known is the reason for which something is done or created or for which something exists, plans may change but purpose is constant, you are designed for your purpose and you are perfect for your purpose. Don't forget that if you don't deploy yourself others will employ you; be what you are because of why you are.

TAKE NOTE #5

—

Health issues

Eyesight is one of the most important senses, with 80 percent of what we perceive coming through our sense of sight. By protecting the eyes you can reduce the odds of blindness and vision loss, while also staying on top of any developing eye disease.

Are certain drinks better for eyesight than others?

It is suggested that certain drinks may be beneficial for eyesight. For example, drinking coffee may help protect against age-related macular degeneration, while consuming sugary drinks may increase the risk of this condition.

Are certain foods better for eyesight than others?

In general, it is advisable to consume a variety of healthy foods and drinks to help maintain good eye health. This includes plenty of fruits, vegetables, and whole grains, as well as moderate amounts of proteins and fats. It is also important to stay hydrated by drinking plenty of water throughout the day.

Are there certain food/drinks you should avoid?

There are no specific foods or drinks that you should avoid maintaining healthy eyesight. However, it is generally recommended to limit your intake of sugary drinks, as they may increase your risk of developing conditions such as diabetes, which can lead to vision problems.

What are some other tips for maintaining eye health?

- Wearing sunglasses or a hat when outdoors to protect your eyes from the sun's harmful UV rays
- Quitting smoking, as tobacco use is a leading cause of preventable blindness
- Exercising regularly, as this can help reduce the risk of developing conditions such as glaucoma
- Getting regular eye exams, as early detection and treatment of eye problems can help prevent vision loss
- Knowing your family history of eye problems, as this can help you be more aware of your own risks.

What are some of the first signs you could have a problem with your eyes?

- Pain or discomfort in the eyes
- Blurred vision
- Changes in vision (e.g. seeing floaters or flashes of light)
- Redness in the eyes
- Tearing or discharge from the eyes

- Swelling or puffiness around the eyes
- Sensitivity to light
- Headaches

If you experience any of these symptoms, it is important to see an optician for a comprehensive eye exam. Early detection and treatment of eye problems can help prevent vision loss. Express Health

CHAPTER 6

Eat The Frog

IF YOU GO TO WORK ON YOUR PLAN, YOUR PLAN WILL GO TO WORK ON YOU. WHATEVER GOOD THINGS WE BUILD, END UP BUILDING US. Jim Rohn

A GOAL IS THE ONGOING PURSUIT OF A WORTHY OBJECTIVE UNTIL ACCOMPLISHED. It seems like every day is a struggle between an endless to-do list and a limited amount of time.

This struggle can make us feel extremely overwhelmed, triggering us into habits that are less than productive and that keep us from getting things done.

When the day ends, we then feel a crushing sense of guilt and anger for not having accomplished what we set out to do. Sounds familiar? Don't despair! One of the ways out is to do one thing at a time. Expect the unexpected. Focus on what you can control and acknowledge what's out of your control.

The shortest way to do many things is to do only one thing at once. Do one thing at a time and do that one thing as if your life depended upon it. Doing just one thing at a time helps you remember more, get more done in less time, de-stress, bring more attention to your work, and work smarter, instead of just harder. It's worth the struggle a hundred times over.

If you are focused on the task at hand the likely hood is that you will be highly productive. Focus on being productive instead of busy. The issue is not knowing what to do; it's doing what you know best.

Ecl. 9:10 - ***Whatsoever thy hand findeth to do, do it with thy might; for there is no work, nor device, nor knowledge, nor wisdom, in the grave, whither thou goest.*** Start by doing what's necessary; then do what's possible; and suddenly you are doing the impossible.

> *All things will be produced in superior quantity and quality, and with greater ease, when each man works at a single occupation, in accordance with his natural gifts, and at the right moment, without meddling with anything else. – Plato*

TAKE NOTE #6

—

Memory Loss

Did you know that memory loss is actually the first sign of brain deterioration?

Research scientist Alan Walker found out the hard way.

When his dad's memory started to go, he turned into a completely different person.

After a long struggle, Alan discovered that the root cause of his father's brain deterioration was something called the BBB.

When your BBB breaks down, your brain neurons are no longer protected and it's only a matter of time until your memory is lost.

But the new discovery at Harvard helps BBB repair itself.

Which is what helped his dad get back to his "old self" again.

Harvard's new discovery is like fountain of youth for your brain. First Health Forum

CHAPTER 7

Swiftly

Create. Not for the money. Not for the fame. Not for the recognition. But for the pure joy of creating something and sharing it. — Ernest Barbaric. I was never really about the money. Every business I've ever started has been more of a curiosity and a kind of "What if?" ... — Blake Mycoskie

When your 'why' is clear and greater than yourself, it will attract other people and resources to support it. Why are you on the planet earth? When you understand your purpose, life will no longer be boring to you. 1 John 3:8 - *He that committeth sin is of the devil; for the devil sinneth from the beginning. For this purpose, the Son of God was manifested, that he might destroy the works of the devil.*

For the past 33 years, I have looked in the mirror every morning and asked myself: 'If today were the last day of my life, would I want to do what I am about to do today?' And whenever the answer has been 'No' for too many days in a row, I know I need to change something. Steve Jobs

But we have to understand why we do what we do, not just do what we do. Vision without action is a daydream. Action without vision is a nightmare. Do what you can right now not sometime later!

You are worthy! Let those words sink deep into your heart. You are worthy. Life can get overwhelming for us, as our busy schedules keep us on our toes. Sometimes we forget that we need to intentionally slow down, take a deep breath, and remind ourselves of our purpose, the very foundation of why we do what we do. When we neglect to quiet our souls and rest in God's amazing grace, we miss out on the intimate opportunities where God assures us of our worthiness, clarifies our purpose, and strengthens us to endure each day. Jennifer E. Smith

You can't make decisions based on fear and the
possibility of what might happen. *Michelle Obama*

Making a quality decision in life to follow your lane, its paramount to your welfare. You cannot please everyone neither can you be everything to everyone. You must recognise your make up and function likewise otherwise you will fumble and crumble.

Stressors are ever present in our lives. In order to achieve more and be more productive, we need to get toxic people and stressors out of our lives. Knowing what your priorities are, focusing on those priorities and getting rid of the weeds in our lives will enhance the quality of our lives and enable us to experience forward momentum.

Ability to say NO will or could add several years to your life; you cannot afford to always be a YES person otherwise you could die before your time. Know and follow your lane, period.

Whether they're family or friends, manipulators are difficult to escape from. Give in to their demands and they'll be happy enough, but if you develop a spine and start saying NO; it will inevitably bring a fresh round of head games and emotional blackmail.

You'll notice that breaking free from someone else's dominance will often result in them accusing you of being selfish. Yes, you're selfish, because you've stopped doing what they want you to do for them. Wow! Can these people hear themselves?! Rosie Blythe,

Understand that you are an EAGLE and not a monkey or a chicken. So, you cannot move with the wrong people and expect to do well. Choose your friends wisely; first and foremost, you must identify toxic people who are currently in your life and ditch them. Don't forget that you are not the Holy Spirit hence you cannot help everyone because you don't have the anointing to do so.

Silence isn't always agreement. Sometimes people no longer argue because they no longer care.

Decision making and problem solving are not the same. To solve a problem, one needs to find a solution. To make a decision, one needs to make a choice. Michael J.

Identify who are potentially the enemies of your forward movement in life and disconnect from them. Let us examine some of those negative influencers that we could come across in our day to day lives, starting from next page.

THE EGOTIST

*Now, let us look at the **EGOTIST**. My candid advice to you is to: **Stay away from lazy parasites, who perch on you just to satisfy their needs, they do not come to alleviate your burdens, hence, their mission is to distract, detract and extract, and make you live in abject poverty.** Michael Bassey Johnson*

The Proud.

Understand that pride sometimes is a virtue; but being arrogant means, you are full of yourself and believe you are superior to everyone around you. You are so full of yourself! You cannot be truly humble, unless you truly believe that life can and will go on without you. MokokomaMokhonoana. Arrogance is a creature. It does not have senses.It has only a sharp tongue and the pointing finger. Toba Beta

A man should have duties outside of himself; without them, he is a mere balloon, inflated with thin egotism and drifting nowhere. Thomas Bailey Aldrich.Being around someone who doesn't treat you with respect but rather intimidates and belittles you can be toxic to your personal development, run from such people.

We cannot negotiate with people who say what's mine is mine

and what's yours is negotiable. [_The Berlin Crisis: Radio and Television_ _Address to the American People_ (The White House, July 25, 1961)] John F. Kennedy. God judge men from the inside out but men on the other hand judges men from the outside in; what a contrast!

Trust your instincts, and make judgments on what your heart tells you. The heart will not betray you. David Gemmell, <u>Fall of Kings</u>

The Envious.

It seems the envious appreciate your difficult times more than your periods of victory. They believe they deserve your moment of success and not you. The motive behind criticism often determines its validity. Those who care criticize where necessary. Those who envy criticize the moment they think that they have found a weak spot. Criss Jami, <u>Killosophy</u>

Don't doubt it; envy comes from wanting something that isn't yours. But grief comes from losing something you've already had. There will be no reason for you to grief this year, In Jesus Mighty Name. Don't panic because God is working behind the scenes; trust Him one more time by casting all your cares on Him for He careth for you. Understand that blessed is the person who has learned to admire but not envy, to follow but not imitate, to praise but not flatter, and to lead but not manipulate; don't be deceived, there are many manipulators out there, please be watchful.

There will always be haters. And the more you grow the more they hate; the more they hate the more you grow. Anthony Liccione. No bird ever looked at a plane in envy. Iain Thomas, 1Corinthians 13:4 - Love is patient, love is kind. It does not envy, it does not boast, it is not proud. Shine your eyes - if the grass is greener on the other side of the fence, please be rest assured that the water bill is higher.

You will hardly find wrong people at right places. Choose to be at the right places and you will find the right people who will inspire you to make it happen! IsraelmoreAyivor. Envious people are dangerous. Cain was envious to the point of murdering his own blood brother!

The Pretentious.

Arrogant men with knowledge make more noise from their mouth than making a sense from their mind.Amit Kalantri, another set of people to watch out for are the Pretentious.

People like these acts as friends when it is comfortable for them to do so; it is always about them and nothing else matters. When you need their help, they tend to depart and stay away. You cannot rely on such people be careful not to become a door mat to such people but do not be bitter nor be unforgiving.We must not hate people, who have done wrong to us. For as soon as we begin to hate them, we become just like them, pathetic, bitter, and untrue. William Shakespeare

Mathew 6:12-15: And forgive us our debts, as we also have forgiven (left, remitted, and let go of the debts, and have given up resentment against) our debtors. And lead (bring) us not into temptation, but deliver us from the evil one. *For Yours is the kingdom and the power and the glory forever. Amen.*

For if you forgive people their trespasses [their reckless and wilful sins, leaving them, letting them go, and giving up resentment], your heavenly Father will also forgive you. But if you do not forgive others their trespasses [their reckless and wilful sins, leaving them, letting them go, and giving up resentment], neither will your Father forgive you your trespasses.

People hate you for three reasons.

- They hate themselves,
- they want to be you,
- or they see you as a threat

The Retrogressive

Mind your mind. Think of distinctive footprints. In so far as all things move forward and not backward, avoid retrogressive thinking, imprison negative thoughts, build a strong wall against negativity, be optimistic enough to deduce the optimisms in pessimism and think ahead of time. Understand the time you have and know what to do with the time, for time can lose it essence with time. If you ignore the real reasons why you wake up each day, you ignore the real reason why you continue to live each day. Life is just once so take the chance and mind your mind.

Ernest AgyemangYeboah

The Retrogressive.

These types' ultimate agenda is to distort your advancement in life and drag you backwards to old habits, (don't forget, it takes thirty days to form a habit). They believe in being stagnant and want you to be the same person you were.

They hate to see you experiencing new level of BREAKTHROUGHS and they will do everything humanly possible to ensure that you are stagnant or retrogress. GUARD YOUR DESTINY, RUN.

This type may be hard to pinpoint, but they are people who have always been an integral part of your life and may seem difficult to ignore. WATCH AND PRAY.

Better ask God to change you, rather than to change your situations for you. Your situations may change, but if you still have a negative attitude, you are likely to take that great change for granted! Change You! **IsraelmoreAyivor,**

Small shifts in your thinking, and small changes in your energy, can lead to massive alterations of your end result

The Judgemental

You become what you digest into your spirit. Whatever you think about, focus on, read about, talk about, you're going to attract more of into your life. Make sure they're all positive. **Germany Kent**

Good day, wonderful people of God. Today is the day the Lord has made and we would rejoice in it on purpose. You must learn how to REJOICE on purpose, RECIRCLE AND REDOUBLE your joy - Nehemiah 8:10 says **the joy of the Lord is my strength.**

Another category of people I want us to look at next are what I called: The **Judgmental**. Don't be surprised that nothing you do is ever good enough for this type of person. They are compulsive critics and in many instances their criticism is not objective but destructive and hurtful. They believe everyone should be criticized and scolded rather than praised.

Criticism has two sides to it; it can make or break us depending on how it is received. You should stop feeling sorry for yourself because your true ability is not limited by the opinions of others. The ultimate goal of a faultfinder is to put you in a box, don't forget that opinions are the cheapest commodity you can find around.

Champions are explorers and performers while faultfinders are passengers, spectators and losers. Self-appointed critics are fools and time wasters. They discuss your past and present you with a gloomy future.

They often explain away your dream based on your past experiences; they take delight in distorting facts. John 2:24-25: 24 But Jesus [for His part] did not trust Himself to them, because He knew all [men]; Jesus did not need anyone to bear witness concerning man [needed no evidence from anyone about men], for He Himself knew what was in human nature. [He could read men's hearts.].Jesus has no time for critics. Self-appointed critics should never be trusted. Do not pay any attention to them because that is the only way to disarm them.

Some people insist that 'mediocre' is better than 'best.' They delight in clipping wings because they themselves can't fly.

The Controller

Take the chair and sit at the fore-front of your dreams. You are the chair-person at the center of affairs; make it memorable; make an impact! Leave a legacy! IsraelmoreAyivor

Let me start by saying that you are a person of purpose; you have a mandate and it is your responsibility to ensure that your DESTINY is fulfilled.

You are already wired to release your potentials thereby making a difference in the world of duplicates. If you don't know your name you will answer to any name and if you don't know where you are going, any road will do. Take charge of your destiny otherwise someone else will do it for you and the outcome could be gloom.

For a control freak, love and the desire to control others are synonymous. Once they lose control over the object of their desire, hostility takes over in full force. Natalya Vorobyova

Let's examine this important issue The Controllers more closely. These set of people are control freak and could be easily found in relationships. They want you to do their bidding. They can be devious, mischievous and sly in trying to twist or out-muscle you to fulfil their desires. Everyone loses their class when they travel through hell. Stay clear of control freaks, they are manipulators and dangerous.

Being a control freak is a weakness, not strength. If you can't allow others to shine, you're exhibiting signs of narcissism and

showing a lack of self-confidence. It is isolation through ego. Stewart Stafford. Romans 16:17-18: <u>Now I beseech you, brethren, mark them which cause divisions and offences contrary to the doctrine which ye have learned; and avoid them.For they that are such serve not our Lord Jesus Christ, but their own belly; and by good words and fair speeches deceive the hearts of the simple.</u>

The Liar

Another set of people to consider next are the **Liars**. Hypocrites get offended by the truth

People who lie frequently can destroy you because in order to grow, you have to surround yourself with trustworthy people who will support you and offer candid and honest opinions. There are different kinds of liars and assume different colours:

Thieves and liars kill indirectly, unintentionally, and with no other weapon than their tongues and malice.A.E.H. Veenman

Colossians 3:9: Do not lie to one another, since you laid aside the old self with its evil practices.

Exodus 23:1: You shall not bear a false report; do not join your hand with a wicked man to be a malicious witness.

There is beauty in truth, even if it's painful. Those who lie, twist life so that it looks tasty to the lazy, brilliant to the ignorant, and powerful to the weak. But lies only strengthen our defects. They don't teach anything, help anything, fix anything or cure anything. Nor do they develop one's character, one's mind, one's heart or one's soul. José N. Harris

Decision is the ultimate power - make the right decision today. You cannot go far in life if you are always a YES person. Do not be too feeble to disconnect some people from your life, otherwise, your life could be upside down instead of you experiencing upward movement in life.

Proverbs 24:28: Do not be a witness against your neighbour without cause, and do not deceive with your lips.

Pigs are dirty, but I will tell you something dirtier: Liars! Untruth always smells like rotten garbage! Mehmet Murat ildan

The Gossiper

The Gossipers. These types of people are dangerous, cancerous and insecure; these people use their tongue to twist facts and distort information. They want to be accepted and recognised and doing so may just be the only way they can get the attention they want.

We have many of such people around us even in religious circles. Please be watchful and protect yourself from these dangerous set of people.

How would your life be different if you walked away from

gossip and verbal defamation? **Let today be the day you speak only the good you know of other people and encourage others to do the same. Steve Maraboli**

Don't base your decisions on the advice of those who don't have to deal with the results. Anonymous. Decisions shape our destinies; wrong decisions can lead you down the wrong path, whereas the right decisions can lead you down the right path.

Do all you can to learn from your bad decisions and improve upon them, as your daily decisions determine the life that you will live. **Stay away from lazy parasites, who perch on you just to satisfy their needs, they do not come to alleviate your burdens, hence, their mission is to distract, detract and extract, and make you live in abject poverty. Michael Bassey Johnson**

Decision to disconnect from people you love and care for might just be almost impossible sometimes but in all you must protect yourself from these sets of people. **Great minds discuss ideas. Average minds discuss events. Small minds discuss people. Henry Thomas Buckle**

A rumour is a social cancer: it is difficult to contain and it rots the brains of the masses. However, the real danger is that so many people find rumours enjoyable. That part causes the infection. Criss Jami, Killosophy

Proverbs 20:19A gossip **betrays a confidence; so avoid anyone who talks too much.**

Every decision brings with it some good, some bad, some lessons,

and some luck. **The only thing that's for sure is that indecision steals many years from many people who wind up wishing they'd just had the courage to leap,** which could help you experience new level of extra-ordinary breakthroughs in life.

The Parasite

Stay away from lazy parasites, who perch on you just to satisfy their needs, they do not come to alleviate your burdens, hence, their mission is to distract, detract and extract, and make you live in abject poverty. Michael Bassey Johnson

The Parasite. These types of people are only in your life to suck you dry and feed off of you. Their intentions are only for their self-interest. They are always inward looking and inward concerning but do not care about others.

They say it takes all kinds to make the world go round, but I can and would love to go without dealing with some. I have come to learn, know, and deal with many different types of people.

While some people come into your life to bring you love, others simply come to teach you a lesson. The people that have taught me the most are actually those that I would consider "parasitic people." Our lives begin to end the day we become silent about things that matter the most. Wise UP, shine your eyes! Refuse to become a door mat. Its time to rise up and occupy your place of honour and power.

Like an actual parasite, they don't always make their presence known right away. More often than not, you welcome them in. Before long, you notice the negative effects they are having on you and those around you, but by that time, it's too late.

In other cases, these parasitic people has been sucking your energy for months or even years. They can be a member of your family or longtime friend that tends to bring out the worst in you, yet you aren't sure how to let go of them or you're used to dealing with their negative behavior. Odyssey

The Victim

Stop validating your victim mentality. Shake off your self-defeating drama and embrace your innate ability to recover and achieve. Dr. Steve Maraboli

Another type of people you must disconnect from immediately are those with **VICTIM mentality.**

The talk of sin is of course to many a big turn-off; to others, an even bigger myth - because in reality, sin is like the spiritual equivalent of a microscopic parasite, or a virus, or better yet even, an infectious disease. And just as one might never know of, until visiting a competent doctor, the tiny pathogens progressively eroding one's body, so we might never know that in sin we are eroding our being and losing direction until hearing the Word of God rightfully applied.......... Criss Jami

The idea that you will forever be the victim of the things that have happened to you is simply nothing but a lie from the pit of hell. Choose to be a victor. The victims never accept responsibility. They are great at pointing their fingers at others and never accepting that they have made errors of judgment in their lives. What chain reaction they cause can have negative impact on your success or breakthrough in life. You must disconnect from such people.

Life is not compassionate towards victims. The trick is not to see yourself as one. It's never too late! I know I've felt like the victim in various situations in my life, but, it's never too late for me to realize that it's my responsibility to stand on victorious ground and know that whatever it is I'm experiencing or going through, those are just the clouds rolling by while I stand here on the top of this mountain! This mountain called Victory! The clouds will come and the clouds will go, but the truth is that I'm high up here on this mountaintop that reaches into the sky! I am a victor. I didn't climb up the mountain, I was born on top of it! **C. JoyBell C**

TAKE NOTE #7

Easy tips to do during your day to set you up for sleep

See the light of day

Our internal clocks are regulated by light exposure. Sunlight has the strongest effect, so try to take in daylight by getting outside or opening the blinds to natural light. Getting a dose of daylight early in the day helps to normalize your circadian rhythm.

Find time to move

Daily exercise has lots of health benefits as you know, and the changes it initiates in energy use and body temperature can promote a solid sleep. We advise against exercise too close to bed time though as this can have a negative effect on your ability to settle down before bed.

Monitor your caffeine intake

Caffeine tricks your brain into thinking it's not tired by blocking your sleepiness signal adenosine. Adenosine is a brain molecule that helps register elapsed time. The longer you are awake, the more adenosine will accumulate in your brain, creating pressure to sleep. Again, caffeine blocks this molecule so you should stop caffeine about 6 hours before bed.

Be mindful of alcohol

Alcohol can induce sleepiness, so some people are keen to get a nightcap before bed. Unfortunately, alcohol affects the brain in ways that lower sleep quality and can inhibit a healthy sleep cycle resulting in your body not actually getting the rest it needs.

Don't eat too late

It can be hard for your body to digest a big dinner. To keep food-based sleep disruptions to a minimum try to avoid late dinners and especially fatty or spicy foods. If you need an evening snack, opt for something light.

Don't smoke

Smoke can cause difficulty falling asleep and is linked to fragmented sleep disorders.

Reserve your bed for sleep and sex only

If you have a comfy bed you may want to lay down in it whilst reading or watching TV but this can actually cause problems at bedtime. You want a strong mental association between your bed and sleep so try to keep activities in your bed limited to sleep and sex.

By SleepAlpha

CHAPTER 8

Desperation versus Determination

No other god can compete with the Creator. When the Lord delivered Israel out of Egypt, he executed judgement against all the gods of Egypt.

Please be reminded that every satanic stronghold will have no choice but to bow to stubborn faith and stubborn prayers.

To conquer frustration, you must remain intensely focused on the outcome of your spiritual engagement with the Holy Spirit and not the obstacles such as spiritual apathy. Don't forget that the miraculous is the hallmark of the Bible and the supernatural is the glue which binds the scriptures together.

If you will permit me, let me ask you this question: Are you desperate or determined? Please note that with desperation comes frustration: Frustration bring about anger, irritability, stress, upset, helplessness, resentment, depression and spiral downward; frustration set in when expectation does not match the efforts you put in. Frustration is very destructive hence you must refuse to be frustrated.

But first and foremost, with determination comes purpose; purpose as you might have known isthe reason for which something is done or created or for which something exists, plans may change but purpose is constant, you are designed for your purpose and you are perfect for your purpose.

Don't forget that if you don't deploy yourself others will employ you; be what you are because of why you are.No matter how you feel – get up, dress up, show up, and never ever give up; you are too loaded to give up.

Do you know that lions only succeed in a quarter of their hunting attempts — which means they fail in 75% of their attempts and succeed in only 25% of them? Despite this small percentage shared by most predators, they don't despair in their pursuit and hunting attempts. The main reason for this is not because of hunger as some might think but it is the understanding of the "Law of Wasted Efforts" that has been instinctively built into animals, a law in which nature is governed. Half of the eggs of fish are eaten... half of the baby bears die before puberty... most of the world's rains fall in oceans... and most of the seeds of trees are eaten by birds. Scientists have found that animals, trees, and other forces of nature are more receptive to the law of "wasted efforts". Only humans think that the lack of success in a few attempts is a failure... but the truth is that: we only fail when we "stop trying".

TAKE NOTE #8

—

Strong Personality

There are signs which shows that you have a strong personality that might scare or intimidatesome people. When people encounter someone with a strong personality, they don't understand the kind of person they are dealing with. Some people think you dominate. Some just think you are rude. But none of these are the truth.

These words actually do not reflect your personality at all. In fact, strong people are often kittens on the inside. It's just that people with domineering personalities just give you a bad rep.Strong people do not have to win, they just are not willing to let other people walk all over them on the outside.Sure, some people might be afraid of you. But that is only because they do not understand how you can be so comfortable with yourself that you do not need anyone else to validate you.

Below are some signs that you have a strong personality that might scare some people.

You Don't Put Up With Excuses: Strong personalities do not put up with excuses. When you have a strong personality, you're not willing to listen to people waste time whining about what they can do. You would rather focus on what you can do and how you can overcome obstacles to do more.

You Are Careful About Who You Let into Your Life: As a strong person, you do not rely on other people to tell you who you are, what you are or what you can do. You recognize that some people need to do that to make themselves feel better. You also recognize that some people need to hear these things to feel whole.

You Hate Small Talk: Small talk is terrible. If you have a strong personality, you have a lot of ideas. You do not want to waste time talking about people when you could be changing the world.

You Can't Stand Insensitivity, Idiocy or Ignorance: Dominating personalities come from a lack of influence or knowledge. Strong personalities are the result of being thoughtful and well-informed. There is a huge difference between the two.

You Know How to Listen: People with strong personalities know how to listen. You might think that people would appreciate this. But in reality, being heard and encouraged actually terrifies people who are not used to it.

You Do Not Need Attention: Having this type of personality means that you do not need attention. Most people that you encounter think that you thrive on it but this is not the truth. It just that your personality attracts people to you. The amount of socializing you do is not because you want to do it but because people need people like you around.

You Are Fearless: Okay, this one is not true. There is probably one thing that you are afraid of. But the difference between you and other people is that you do not let this fear dictate the way you live your life.

You Take Insecurity As An Opportunity: Insecurity for you is an opportunity to do better. You know you're not perfect but if you are not trying to learn and evolve, despite the risk of looking like a fool, then you are not living. You are just existing.

They say everyone is insecure and this is probably true. But not everyone has to stop this insecurity from letting them live their life and own the things that they are insecure about.

Sure, some people think that people with big personalities are difficult to be around. But you're only difficult to be around because you challenge other people to be the best version of themselves! If this is what being difficult is like than you already know that it is best to just keep being you. <u>Michael Prywes</u>

CHAPTER 9

Wattage

The universe is wired with the electricity of God and each of us is a lamp. It doesn't matter the size or shape of the lamp; it only matters that the lamp is plugged in. With every prayer, every thought of forgiveness, every meditation, every act of love, we plug in. The more of us who plug in, the more the darkness of the world will be cast from our midst. Today, let's all increase love's wattage! Marianne Williamson

Ephesians 2:10 – For we are His workmanship, created in Christ Jesus unto good works, which God hath before ordained that we should walk in them. You are a child of God and you can believe this as a fact when you get to know Him more intimately. To know God more intimately, you have to get glued to His Word, read and study the Word over and over again.

I believe the words of the Psalmist will warm your heart. Psalm

34:1 – I will bless the Lord at all times; His praise shall continually be in my mouth. If the praise of God is continually in your mouth, you cannot give credit to the devil for anything. The devil is already a defeated foe and he cannot recover from his defeat and destruction.

Do not be afraid of the evil one another day of your life. Psalm 34:2 – My soul shall make its boast in the Lord; the humble shall hear of it, and be glad. I ask you today, who are you going to boast about? Or what will you boast about? Certainly, it should not be centred on self-glorification.

Remember: He WANTS your fellowship, and He has done everything possible to make it a reality. He has forgiven your sins, at the cost of His own dear Son. He has given you His Word, and the priceless privilege of prayer and worship. **Never take your obedience as the reason God blesses you; obedience is the outcome of being rightly related to God**

Jesus taught that your highest priority must be your relationship with Him. If anything, distracts you from that relationship, that activity is not from God. God will not ask you to do something that hinders your relationship with Christ.

Romans 14:23 – Whatever is not of faith is sin. You will agree with me that fear is not of faith. Fear is the opposite of faith. Psalm 34:4 – I sought the Lord, and He heard me, and delivered me from all my fears.

You are promised in the Word of God that you are delivered from all fears – fear of rejection, fear of failure, fear of poverty, fear of sickness, fear of the future, anxiety about the past, etc.

Fear is deadly. Fear of failure does grip many people. I Chronicles 28:20 says – Be strong and courageous and get to work. Do not be frightened by the size of the task, for the Lord my God is with you: He will not forsake you. Fear paralyses but faith strengthens!

He will see to it that everything is finished correctly. God helped Zerubbabel to complete what he began - be rest assured that if God has done it before He will do it again and again. Zechariah 4:8, 9 - *Moreover the word of the Lord came to me, saying: "The hands of Zerubbabel have laid the foundation of this [a]temple; His hands shall also finish it, then you will know that the Lord of hosts has sent me to you.*

Stubborn, rebellious, stiff-necked people miss the great things God has for them because they refuse to let God work in them. He is working on those who let Him because He will never force Himself on people. God is not a gate crasher. Revelation 3:20 reveals that we must open the door of our hearts and allow Jesus to work in us. Sometimes He comforts us but at other times He convicts, rebukes and corrects us. Honesty is the key as far as God is concerned so **don't worry about having the right words; concern yourself more about having the right heart. It's not eloquence that matters to Him**

Weak people revenge. Strong people forgive. Intelligent people ignore. You cannot go to the top if you always care what another think. You decide either you find a way or create a way; but you cannot afford to create an excuse. My candid advice to you today is that you shouldn't try to be anyone but you. Each of us is unique and our highest and best is to be precisely and fully who we are made to be by the Almighty God; yes, the ever loving, Daddy above.

A tree does not make a forest neither does anyone has monopoly of wisdom hence we can all learn from others. Unfortunately, too often we learn accidentally and bad habits too easily find room in our lives. But we can also learn intentionally from the most successful and inspiring people we can find. Choose your models wisely; your life depends on it, beloved in Christ.How passionate are you about you reason for being?

Always remember that there can be no two of you, otherwise one of you is unnecessary. God works in your life proportionate to your passion for Him. God cannot be mocked whatsoever a man soweth that shall he also reap; with God no short cut. God has never responded to potential. He never works in your life relative to your need of Him.

Big Daddy above always responds to passion. He is not overly impressed by what He gives you. He responds to your reaction to the gift. What you do with the gifts He stored in you decides the favour of God.

Big Daddy above gives talent but work transforms talent into genius. Happiness comes from clarity. It comes from deciding who we are, what we value, and how we will spend our lives. And that comes from taking time to think clearly, make smart choices, and plan wisely for wisdom is the principal thing therefore we must crave for wisdom.

The key to Christian living is a thirst and hunger for God. To hunger is to have a strong desire or craving for something. It's that gnawing ache on the inside of you; that sense of need that is not content until it is filled.

And hunger for God is the landing strip of the Holy Spirit; it is a signal that God is setting you up for an encounter with Him! Newness, for something new is on the horizon—but before you step into your destiny, it's time to catch a fresh revelation of who Jesus is. And deepen your relationship with Him. Hear Him saying, **"I want to feast with you. I want to share all that I am with you." - Rev 3:20)**

Evidence of hunger for God

Ditching Status Quo

Hunger for God is often characterized by a feeling of discontent. You sense you are missing something in your relationship with the Big Daddy above. You are no longer satisfied with the degree to which you have known Jesus. You begin to feel restless in that discontent, for the Holy Spirit is drawing you closer to Him.

Previous Experience

You remember a past encounter with God, and it stirs hunger in you. You may find yourself yearning for what is behind—the "good old days" of faith. If you can relate to this, know that what you have tasted before, can be yours again—and more! That longing you have—that hunger—is setting you up for what is to come.

Spiritual Fatigue

Awareness of your own spiritual weakness can be painful. But within that trial you're in right now, is an invitation from the Big Daddy above. For God has a new strength for you, that can only be found in Him. In

Him you are able to do all things; don't forget that the key to Christian living is a thirst and hunger for the Big Daddy above.

Exceptional People

The hallmark of successful people is cheerful optimism, attempting something new, flexible, doing stuff, learning stuff, never lazy about, proactiveness, constantly moving forward are the most fundamental traits of successful people. The Bible says he that does not work must not eat, that is a divine order. Winners Choose Optimism, Every Time.

What is the biggest, most important key to success in life? Attitude! Remember the old saying that "Your attitude determines your altitude?" I'm convinced it's true.

Optimism comes naturally and easily to only a few. Perhaps they are wired differently, I don't know. But for the majority of people, optimism is a learned skill, a chosen approach to life. It's a conscious decision to see "the glass as half-full." Clearly, this is a troubled world and there are lots of problems out there, Ukraine war among many others; We can't deny the gloominess covering the world right now! But it's also true that, "what we focus on, expands." And, of course, "we become what we think about most of the time." Proverbs 23:7 *says as a man thinketh in his heart so is he.*

If you don't like something, change it. If you can't change it, change your attitude. Even in tough times, we are rich beyond our imagination! And yet the news is almost uniformly bad, bloody and painful most especially with Covid 19 – We worry all day long (at the time of writing this book we have about 300,000 infections per day, in

UK) but Ukraine war means that emphasise is no longer on Covid-19 as all restrictions are no longer in place.

Hence, people are angry, discouraged, and actively practicing their "victim "approach to life. Always remind yourself that you are not a VICTIM but a VICTOR through the blood of Jesus Christ which He shed on the CROSS for you and me. **Sooner or later, those who win are those who think they can.** High achievers refuse to buy into this negativity! Winners have always looked for the good, emphasised hope, and found opportunity where others see only problems. What do you see? What you see is what possess you and that will either take you to the top of the pyramid of life or tie you to the bottom of the pyramid of life - it's your decision.

Apathy makes excuses while passion finds a way. Exceptional people don't make excuses but always find a way where it means there is no way. We are to display the politics of heaven on earth. Dear reader, give it time, Big Daddy above is at work underground hence stop trying to force fruit that is not yet due. You can be intelligent and talented without reaching the top. Until you make up your mind never to quit, you will remain a part of 95% of group of people who never tasted success.

Don't partner with mediocrity which is below average; stop mourning and complaining about how life had treated you because the world is not blessed by talkers but by people who are determined to make success out of it. In each of us are places where we have never gone only by pressing the limits do you ever find them. Pride must die in you or nothing of heaven can live in you. Admit you cannot accomplish your goals by your power or intellect but rather lean on the Big Daddy above. Apostle Paul said in first Corinthians chapter sixteen verse nine – For a great door and effectual is opened unto me, and there are many adversaries. Every opposition is contending for your position hence you must endure against all odds and success will be the outcome. The lazy cannot go far as they are set for fumbling and stumbling.

Pride will cost you everything but leave you with nothing. Spiritual arrogance is dangerous never join the foolish ones to play such a game. Admit you are not adequate in yourself; you need the Big Daddy above and we all do. Don't forget that the struggles we endure today will be the 'good old days' we laugh about tomorrow.

Desire is the key to motivation, but it is determination and commitment to an unrelenting pursuit of your goal - a commitment to excellence - that will enable you to attain the success you seek. Resilience requires optimism and strength. Patience is bitter, but its fruit is sweet. They that wait on the Big Daddy above will ultimately renew their strength.

Successful people do not major on taking without a deposit. There are two kinds of people on earth - the TAKERS and the GIVERS. Who are you between the two; *a taker or a giver*? The takers may eat better, but the givers sleep better. It is good to be generous but please don't set yourself on fire to keep others warm. Jesus died for us all but there will be no second cruxification.

We come to realise that successful people are always looking for opportunities to help others. Unsuccessful people are always asking, 'what is in it for me?' However, when givers indulge in a connection, there is a spark; it is alchemy. It is a situation of I water you, you water me, we never drain each other, we just grow together. Relationship is 'give' and 'take.'

We must be like the Big Daddy above - who gives perpetually and He is never tired of giving. *Are you a giver or a taker?* Professional takers are parasites because they never give anything back.

John 3:16 - *For God so greatly loved and dearly prized the world that He [even] gave up His only begotten ([a]unique) Son, so that*

whoever believes in (trusts in, clings to, relies on) Him shall not perish (come to destruction, be lost) but have eternal (everlasting) life.

Some main characteristics of givers and takers are:

- Givers understand reality and human need takers prefer fantasy and meeting their own needs
- Givers want to be accountable, responsible citizens but takers really don't want to account to anyone or have many responsibilities
- Givers realize they may have to wait to get what they want or even do without but takers live by the law of instant gratification
- Givers look out for their families but takers look out for themselves
- Givers stick with a marriage when the going gets tough but takers bail out because they are not being fulfilled.

Marketers

Good marketing makes the company look smart. Great marketing makes the customer feel smart. I am all for conversations, but you need to have a message; what is your message? Acts 1:8 – But you shall receive power when the Holy Spirit has come upon you; and you shall be [a]witnesses to Me in Jerusalem, and in all Judea and Samaria, and to the end of the earth.
Joe Chernov

All Christians are expected to be marketers. Marketing for Big Daddy above and His beloved Son is profitable and well rewarding. Mothers do not care about the labour pains they are interested only in seeing the baby; you are challenged to give birth to your dreams: Make it happen.

Making noise about the goodness of God and the price Jesus paid on the cross for everyone in the world. *For God so loved the world that He gave His only begotten Son, that whoever believes in Him should not perish but have everlasting life.* There are thirteen times in the Bible where we are commanded to shout, and tremendous things happen when you get your voice lifted up and you begin to shout to the Lord.

Don't be a whisperer Christian, but let your voice be heard. Psalm

47:1 - O Clap your hands, all ye people; shout unto God with the voice of triumph. Shout and let people hear your voice.

We must be vocal Christians – alive Christians. I believe God is raising up an army of shouters in these last days. Do not be ashamed of your obligations in Christ, shout with all pleasure. Psalm 51:11 - *But let all those rejoice who put their trust in you; let them ever shout for joy.* Psalm 32:11 – **Be glad in the Lord and rejoice, you righteous; and Shout for joy, all you upright in heart.**

Starbucks

Change cannot be avoided... change provides the opportunity for innovation. It gives you the chance to demonstrate your creativity. Live with intention. Walk to the edge. Listen hard. Practice wellness. Play with abandon. Laugh. Choose with no regret. Do what you love. Live as if this is all there is. Mary Anne Radmacher

Whether you're grieving the loss of a loved one or are adjusting to moving to a new place, life is full of uncertainty. Navigating previously unexplored terrain is difficult, exhausting, and even scary. Change is the only constant thing in life. Spanish Proverb says - *A wise man changes his mind, a fool never will.*

Physical relocation doesn't change who you are. It only changes the view outside your window. If you want to fly, you have to give up what weighs you down. Change the way you look at things and the things you look at change, it may be that the problem lies with you and not your spouse. Self-examination is always very useful. Until you turn the page you will never know what the next page contains. Change is painful, but nothing is as painful as staying stuck somewhere you don't belong. All things are difficult before they are easy.

John 16:33 says - *These things I have spoken to you, that in Me you may have peace. In the world you [a]will have tribulation; but be of good cheer, I have overcome the world.* Every day the clock resets.

Your wins don't matter. Your failures don't matter. Don't stress on what was, fight for what could be – tomorrow will be better, your best days are not behind you but before you. Don't let rejection create self-doubt. The founder of Starbucks was turned down by 217 of the 242 investors he initially spoke with. If you don't believe in your dreams no one will!

Tracking

Not long ago we sent a document to Kenya to our lawyer in Nairobi through Parcelforce to enable him perfect the purchase of a landed property for the work we do in the country. The document was not delivered on time so we kept tracking the document until it was delivered.

You must learn to track the progress you are making on the journey of your life. Engage your gear as putting it in neutral could hinder your progress in life. Key into your imagination; imagination is the highest kite that one can fly. How often do you key into your imagination? Most people key more into the realm of memory which replays the past than for them to key into the realm of imagination which pre-plays the future.

Ephesians 3:20 - **Now to Him who is able to do exceedingly abundantly above all that we ask or think, according to the power that works in us.** The truth of the matter is that every man dies. Not every man truly lives.

Just as it is essential to know the difference between working hard and working smart, so we must understand the difference between creating something big, and creating something meaningful. The difference between goals, dreams, hopes and fantasies is by tracking progress. Dreams and wishes are fantastic fun.

They have the capacity to inspire you and they let you escape to a world where everything is wonderful. Goals, on the other hand, are pesky. Yes, they are fun because they determine your future, but they require a whole different set of skills and commitments. Commitment to your calling in life should never be negotiable.

Goals require planning and discipline. ***Be patient with yourself*** because ***Self-growth is tender.*** Goals require a reasonable way to "get there." Goals should make you think, solve problems, and often require teamwork or partnership with others. Goals demand measurement. With dreams, hopes and fantasies, you can work on them when you feel like it. Sometimes, you could enjoy the dream so much that you don't actually do anything to make it happen hence it doesn't create results and it rarely changes your life in a dramatic way. Goals, on the other hand, require work and steady, predictable progress.

Repulsiveness

The arrogant person always wants to do the right thing, the great thing. But because he wants to do it in his own strength, he is fighting not with man, but with Big Daddy. *A proud man is always looking down on things and people; and, of course, as long as you are looking down, you cannot see something that is above you.* At every stage of our Christian development, and in every sphere of our Christian discipleship, pride is our greatest enemy and humility our greatest friend. This nasty attitude was displayed in Genesis chapter eleven verses one to four: And the whole earth was of one language and of one speech. And it came to pass, as they journeyed from the east, that they found a plain in the land of Shinar; and they dwelt there. And they said one to another, Go to, let us make brick, and burn them thoroughly. And they had brick for stone, and slime had they for mortar. Now the next verse is the interesting bit: And they said, Go to, let us build us a city and a tower, whose top may reach unto heaven; and let us make us a name .... lest we be scattered abroad upon the face of the whole earth.

Antidotes to repulsiveness

First, upward looking in thanksgiving unto God; The Psalmist knows how to do this effectively. Thankfulness stops pride growing. Thankfulness is a sign of a born again Christian while ingratitude… [Is] one of the distinguishing marks of those who do not retain God in their hearts. The fool says Big Daddy does not exist.

An attitude of gratitude brings great things." "We must find the time to stop and thank the people who make a difference in our lives." "Reflect upon your present blessings, of which every man has plenty; not on your past misfortunes, of which all men have some." Gratitude unlocks the fullness of life. Be thankful. Be present in all things and thankful for all. In the constant act of thanksgiving, the relationship with Big Daddy is nurtured and strengthened.

Avoid victim mentality because such an attitude will hinder you from recognising the things Big Daddy has done for you and hence thank Him for them. Be thankful for what you have; you'll end up having more. If you concentrate on what you don't have, you will never, ever have enough. *Pride slays thanksgiving, but a humble mind is the soil out of which thanks naturally grow. A proud man is seldom a grateful man, for he never thinks he gets as much as he deserves.*

One of the antidotes of repulsiveness is to confess our sins the moment we missed the mark; please understand that confession is a reality check as it reminds us who we are. If Big Daddy did not forgive the Christian who confesses and turns away from sin then Big Daddy will become unrighteous by holding in contempt Christ's atoning work, whose purpose was to uphold God's glory.

Believers' confession need not be overwhelming because the cross was sufficient for all our sins and we have been completely forgiven. Jesus did not go to the cross in vain as He paid the price of sin in full. It is at the cross that we understand most clearly that we are sinners, but it is also at the cross that we understand most clearly that we are deeply loved. Big Daddy's compassion for mankind cannot be explained! Too much love; excess love. The grace must not be taking for granted. The grace must not be abused. Cheap grace is the preaching of forgiveness without requiring repentance, baptism without church discipline, Communion without confession, absolution without personal confession. Cheap grace is grace without discipleship, grace without the cross, and grace without Jesus Christ.

When we confess, we gain a deeper appreciation of grace and what we have been saved from. Big Daddy above's forgiveness gives us peace and security, and therefore the freedom to grow in humility. 1 John 1:7-10 - *but if we walk in the light, as he is in the light, we have fellowship one with another, and the blood of Jesus Christ his Son cleanses us from all sin. If we say that we have no sin, we deceive ourselves, and the truth is not in us. If we confess our sins, he is faithful and just to forgive us our sins, and to cleanse us from all unrighteousness. If we say that we have not sinned, we make him a liar, and his word is not in us. Forgiveness is always free. But that does not mean that confession is cheap or easy ride.*

Repulsive attitude can be tamed. Learn to promote others instead focusing on yourself always; it's not always about you. Self-glorification is dangerous.

Stop self-glorifying and give back the glory to Big Daddy above in everything you do. Let humility characterized your life. People who are humble inspire trust and confidence in those around them, and therefore humility is key for leadership.

Self-glorification first of all is a very serious matter. Many believers have been sucked and deceived into thinking that the ultimate desire or purpose on earth is to excel above everyone else in any given field. That is what the world conforms to. Glorifying self invites the world to watch us; glorifying Big Daddy invites angels to guard us. The more people notice us, the less angels protect us.

The greatest edifice that we can erect to ourselves is to give ourselves over to building the edifices within other people in a manner that they might carry a part of ourselves, but they look nothing like ourselves.

Nastiness or Pride is anti-social behaviour, whereas when we're humble, it's best for others and best for us, as it's who we were created and redeemed to be. You will never glory in Big Daddy above till first of all God has killed your glorying in yourself. Self-obsession can be so bad. Self-focus is self-deceiving.

Proverbs 6:17 - *These six things the Lord hates, yea, seven are an*

abomination to Him. A proud look, a lying tongue, and hands that
shed innocent blood, An heart that deviseth wicked imaginations,
feet that be swift in running to mischief, a false witness that speaketh
lies, and he that soweth discord among brethren.

There are more things you can do to help mitigate against pride or nasty behaviour. Do your best to live a life of humility since arrogance is the armour of the weak. They are always at war to hide their real self. Humility is not thinking less of yourself but thinking of yourself less. A humble person is naturally a carrier of tremendous grace.

Dear reader, if you have a sense of humour and you can laugh at yourself which means not taking yourself too seriously it might help to swallow your pride. Everyone has a sense of humour. If you don't laugh at jokes, you probably laugh at opinions. A sense of humour is the best indicator that you will recover; it is often the best indicator that people will love you; it means we can more quickly admit we're wrong. It means we're more real.

Do not assume monopoly of wisdom. Do not look down on others. Do not prove too, know. When we listen to people it's a sign of love, of wisdom, and shows that we're teachable, and it's a way we can become humbler. Stop complaining as none of us is without difficulties either in low or high life.

Seek counsel from others. Listening to others is an indication that we are willing to learn from them. Ask questions, seek for information. When we ask questions with the right attitude and manner it shows we recognize we don't have all the answers. Know your limitations because none of us is perfect.

The realisation of imperfection will help us to humble ourselves. One of the basic rules of the universe is that nothing is perfect. Perfection simply doesn't exist.... Without imperfection, neither you nor I would exist. Imperfections are not inadequacies; they are reminders that we're all in this together. Life is not always perfect. Like a road, it has many bends, ups and down, but that's its beauty. Practice doesn't make perfect. Practice reduces the imperfection.

- Poverty reduces a MAN to a boy, a WOMAN to a girl!

- Its only Success that can turn your Mockers to your Workers!

- Salary is a Short Term solution to a Long Term Problem!

- Show me a man who never takes Risk and I'll show you a man who never accomplishes Anything!

- Poverty does not die by fire. It dies by calculated Hard Work!

- You cannot cast a Six(6) except you throw a Dice!

- Nothing is worse than Missing an Opportunity that would have Changed Your Life!

- Don't be a POOR man who Passes Over Opportunity Repeatedly!

- When you see People who are making Money Genuinely, join them. Too much Analysis leads to Paralysis!

- The more Excuses you make the Lesser the money in your Pocket!

- Be Wise.

TAKE NOTE #9

—

Make sleep a priority using these four simple BUT effective steps.

1. Stick to the same bed-time every night ensuring you have at least 9 hours until you have to wake.

2. Practice a relaxing pre-bed-time routine to make it easier to fall asleep - this should be relaxing for you and should be something that's calming and does not conflict with point 3!

3. Disconnecting from electronic devices 1 hour before bed - it really works, 'blue light' and all that....

4. Keep it **DARK**! When you do go to sleep, keep it as dark as possible. If its light in your room at night this just sends a signal to your brain that it isn't quite time to sleep.

Confused mind is a sleepless mind.

Do this for more than 1 week to get into a routine. **DO NOT** just do it for 2-3 days then give up because it appears ineffective, give it time and give it a chance. Obviously as always, no caffeine 8 hours before bed and sleep in a cool room not a hot room.

SleepAlpha

CHAPTER 10

Stay Radiant

O nly 8% of our worry will come to pass. 92% of our worry is wasted. DON'T PANIC. Mark Gorman. It is difficult to live in and enjoy the moment when you are thinking about the past or worrying about the future. Roy Bennett.

Psalm 16:8 - I have set the Lord always before me.
Because He is at my right hand, I will not be shaken

Do not be deluded by expecting an overnight success because it will not happen. We can say with a high degree of certainty that it is going to take hard work and dedication to achieve your goals. Please be aware that there is no free lunch anywhere.

Accept the fact that there is no yellow brick road to your dreams hence a price must be paid in full. It doesn't matter if you're trying to be an engineer or an accountant or a social worker or a teacher or a coffee shop owner. The trials and tribulations are what make you feel successful when your dreams turn into reality.

A stupid man stays awake all night pondering his problems; he's worn out when morning comes and whatever was, still is. Poems of the Elder Edda

Wasting energy on worry is like carrying an umbrella around in the desert because it just might rain. Clyde Lee Dennis. Worrying, trying harder, and always feeling like you are falling short is the opposite of God's will for your life. God does not want your effort: He wants your obedience Marnie Swedberg,

It is better to worship than worry. Lailah Gifty Akita.

Faith is the ability to believe in what we cannot see, but what is true. Worry is the opposite of faith. It believes in what does not exist, except in our fears. It's like we have bought into an illusion that does not serve us, makes us ill, binds us in fear, causes us to procrastinate, and limits our progress. Cristie B. Gardner.

Do not let your CONCERNS becomes your CARES, and your FORETHOUGHTS to become your FEAR- THOUGHTS. There is no need to get worried about anything and that does not imply that you do not care about what is going on in your surroundings.

You must put a Lid on Your Worrying Sometimes we stress endlessly about negative experiences when just walking away from them would serve us far better. You must refuse to be stressed out because you are the one in control.

Worrying about that which has already happened is like trying to saw sawdust! Worrying about the past is like trying to put toothpaste back into the tube. Past deeds cannot be undone or past words unsaid.

Worry is itself an illness, since worry is an accusation against Divine Wisdom, a criticism of Divine Mercy. Said Nursi. . Worry divides the mind. If you want to be happy, do not dwell in the past, do not worry about the future, focus on living fully in the present. We would worry less if we praised more. Thanksgiving is the enemy of discontent and dissatisfaction.

People of God, when you think your life is over, a new story line falls and lands right in your lap and boom! A change is birthed in your life. Don't worry about not getting "it" perfectly right now. It's ok, just keep at it, you will soon settle in it and then you'll be glad you didn't give up, that is the way to move to the next level in life.

Sorrow looks back, worry looks around, faith looks up. Ralph Waldo Emerson. Learn to celebrate today, thank God for today, cherish today and live for today, whatever happened in the past or that might happen in the future must not intrude upon today, it's your season, grab it with both hands.

Stop your whining. If you are frightened, be silent. Whining is for prey. It attracts predators. And you are not prey. Robin Hobb. You are challenged today to ditch worrying. That will help you make a worryfree environment. Plato knew that the body and mind are intimately linked. And in the late 1800s, the Mayo brothers, famous physicians, estimated that over half of all hospital beds are filled with people suffering from frustration, anxiety, worry and despair. Causes of worry are everywhere, in our relationships and our jobs, so it's key we find ways to take charge of the stress.

Worry never robs tomorrow of its sorrow, it only saps today of its joy. Leo F. Buscaglia Our fatigue is often caused not by work, but by worry, frustration and resentment. Dale Carnegie.Listen, it is difficult to live in and enjoy the moment when you are thinking about the past or worrying about the future. You cannot change your past, but you can ruin the present by worrying about your future. Cast your burdens upon the Lord, today.

Worrying is carrying tomorrow's load with today's strength-carrying two days at once. It is moving into tomorrow ahead of time. Worrying doesn't empty tomorrow of its sorrow, it empties today of its strength. Corrie Ten Boom.

Worry is like a rocking chair: it gives you something to do but never gets you anywhere. Erma Bombeck. The more you pray, the less you'll panic. The more you worship, the less you worry. You'll feel more patient and less pressured. Rick Warren.

TAKE NOTE #10

—

Principles of Effective Goal Setting

G oal setting is an essential practice for living a happy and fulfilling life. Goals provide you with purpose, direction, and motivation. They give you something to strive for, and they force you to change and improve yourself to achieve them.

Back in 1990, Professors Edwin Locke and Gary Latham published <u>A Theory of Goal Setting and Task Performance</u>, in which they identified five principles of effective goal setting:

- Clarity
- Challenge
- Commitment
- Feedback
- Task Complexity

Basically, if you follow these tips, you will be much more likely to set effective goals and achieve them.

Let's take a closer look at these unspoken principles of goal setting.

- **Set Clear and Concise Goals:** The first principle discussed by Locke and Latham was clarity. This means your goal should be very well defined and not be unclear or vague. You should be able to picture exactly what your life would look like after you achieve your goal and when you want it to happen. Unclear goals are a recipe for fumbling around, hitting roadblocks, and never really achieving what you want.

- After all, how do you know if you've accomplished a goal if you never really knew what you were after? Having something concrete and measurable not only makes achieving your goals more likely, but also makes it much easier to track progress along the way.

- **Make Your Goals Challenging:** "If you want to be happy, set a goal that commands your thoughts, liberates your energy and inspires your hopes." -Andrew Carnegie. Having a clear and concise goal isn't enough to make it an effective one. It's nearly as important to make sure that <u>the goal you set for yourself is also challenging</u>. It should be enough to test your character and make you feel like you've really accomplished something. When engaging in goal setting, your goals have to be something worth fighting for. Research from Locke and Latham indicates that challenging goals inspire increased performance. Meaning the level of effort you put in is directly related to the difficulty of the goal.

- Truly and Deeply Commit to Your Goals: People perform better when they care about what they're doing and why they're doing it, and the same applies to goal setting. Try to think about the tasks you accomplish on a day-to-day basis at work. Which ones do you put the most effort into and which ones do you as quickly as possible just to finish them? It's the emotional commitment to your goals that gives you the motivation you need to accomplish them. To be successful, you need to make sure <u>the goals you set</u> are something you truly want and can fully be on board with in the short term.

- Review Feedback on Your Progress: "Goal setting is

most effective when there is feedback showing progress in relation to the goal." According to Prof. Edwin Locke. In the process of goal setting, you need to have feedback along the way to ensure you're staying on track and making progress towards your goal, and to take stock of what's working and what's not.Set some time aside every so often to step back, review your goals, and track your progress. Doing so will help you hit your mark and keep you motivated along the way.

- Break Down Complex Tasks Into Simpler Tasks: If you've followed the second principle and set a challenging goal for yourself, it will probably have many complex tasks associated with its achievement. These tasks can be daunting and extremely overwhelming, especially when starting with a stack a mile high.You have to break down these daunting tasks systematically into simpler, less-complicated tasks that are easier to approach and overcome when goal setting.

CHAPTER 11

PUSH PULL HARD

Samuel Jackson

The famous movie star was 46 when he played his role as Jules Winnfield in *Pulp Fiction*. Before then, Jackson had struggled with drug addiction for two years until he got his first major role in *Jungle Fever* in 1991.

Martha Stewart

Stewart worked in catering for years, but her role as "America's housewife" did not materialize until she started writing cookbooks and other pieces on domestic living in her 40s.

Ronald Reagan

Reagan obviously had a successful acting career, but he first came onto the political stage when he delivered his famous "A Time for Choosing" speech during the 1964 election at the age of 53. He leveraged his past acting talents to become one of the most respected presidents of the 20th century.

Henry Ford

In his youth, Ford worked as an engineer under Thomas Edison, where he worked on ways to improve the then new automobile. It was not until he was 40 that he founded the Ford Motor company, where he introduced the Model T five years later.

Abraham Lincoln

At the age of 40, Lincoln left the House of Representatives and went back to practicing law, his young political career seemingly over. He jumped onto the just-founded Republican Party seven years later, and then was elected President of the United States four years after that.

Reid Hoffman

Not every social media website was founded by some young tech genius. Reid Hoffman founded SocialNet.com in 1997, a precursor of sorts to Facebook. But he founded LinkedIn in 2002 at age 35, and then worked for years to make it the professional social networking site. When Hoffman took LinkedIn public 8 years later, he became a billionaire.

Lee Ermey

Ermey's infamous performance as Gunnery Sergeant Hartman in *Full Metal Jacket* was his first major acting role at the age of 43. Ermey was originally supposed to be an advisor, but was cast as Hartman by impressing Stanley Kubrick with his knowledge of life as a Marine.

Ray Kroc

Kroc worked various jobs including a pianist and a travelling salesman for a milkshake maker. Then at the age of 52, he met the McDonalds brothers and proposed that their restaurant could expand across the United States. By the time he died in 1984, McDonald's had become well, McDonald's become well known.

Richard Adams

While he worked as a British civil servant, Adams told his two daughters a story about a rabbit, who insisted that he write it down. After writing it down two years later, he published *Watership Down*, which instantly became a children's literary classic.

Jack Cover

Cover worked for NASA and IBM, and eventually used his scientific knowledge to create a weapon which could stop individuals without killing them. Today, police agencies across the world use his Taser to subdue criminals nonviolently.

Momofuku Ando

As Japan recovered from the end of World War II, Ando sought a way to provide quick and cheap noodles to his impoverished countrymen. At the age of 48, Ando developed the instant ramen which sustains college students everywhere.

Alan Rickman

Rickman quit a successful graphic design business in his mid-20s to go into acting, but spent years working in theater until he was asked to play the role of Hans Gruber in *Die Hard.*

Sam Walton

Walton ran several stores, and failed many times in the process. But he learned from those failures and used the lessons to open the first Wal-Mart at 44 and become one of the richest men in the world. The store's philosophy was simple, buy in bulk and sell them cheap. Today his stores sell everything from groceries to electric skateboards, and everything in between.

Miguel de Cervantes

Widely credited as the first Western novelist for his work *Don Quioxte,* Cervantes did not publish his first book until 38 and his most famous work at 58. Before then, he served in the Spanish Navy and struggled for years to find work which could support him as he wrote.

Julia Child

The woman who brought French cuisine to American televisions did not eat French food until she was 36, working for the OSS in post-war France. But after being absolutely stunned by French food, she studied the cuisine fanatically until she had enough knowledge to host *The French Chef* at 51.

Colonel" Harland Sanders

Sanders worked a variety of odd jobs throughout his life, and watched his first attempt at a fried chicken restaurant fail at the ripe old age of 65. But Sanders used his Social Security checks to begin franchising Kentucky Fried Chicken, which became the success it is today.

Tim and Nina Zagat

These two certainly enjoyed success throughout their life as a pair of corporate lawyers. But after making a list of local restaurants they liked or did not like; they expanded the list into a full-time business. Today, the Zagat list covers over 70 cities.

Charles Darwin

Darwin went on his famous voyage on the HMS Beagle at just 21, but his work as a naturalist was held back by health issues. It was not until he was 50 that he finally published *On the Origin of Species.*

Peter Mark Roget

Peter Mark Roget had an interest in lists and orderly language throughout his life. When he retired from his scientific and mechanical work in 1840 at the age of 61, he began preparing to work on a book which would organize words by their definitions. The first thesaurus was published in 1852.

Grandma" Moses

Anna Moses loved to embroider, but when her fingers started to fail at the age of 78, she took up painting. Today, she is remembered as one of America's great folk artists, who painted scene after scene of American rural life. By Michael Prywes

CHAPTER 12

Excess Love

John 3:16 - For God so loved the world, that He gave His only begotten Son, that whosoever believeth in Him should not perish, but have everlasting life. There is no doubt that the Big Daddy above is too good and awesome beyond comprehension. He loves us extraordinarily; the best way to describe His love for mankind is: EXCESS LOVE.

Shannon Alder says: He is worthy of trust. There will always be someone willing to hurt you, put you down, gossip about you, belittle your accomplishments and judge your soul. It is a fact that we all must face. However, if you realize that God is a best friend that stands beside you when others cast stones you will never be afraid, never feel worthless and never feel alone.

When everything's changing around you, it's important to remember that the Big Daddy above is a constant and consistent Father. He will never let you down. He can be counted on. He is a reliable Father and dependable too; He is the Rock of Ages. Though we are incomplete, God loves us completely. Though we are imperfect,

He loves us perfectly. Though we may feel lost and without compass, God's love encompasses us completely. ... He loves every one of us, even those who are flawed, rejected, awkward, sorrowful, or broken. James chapter one verse seventeen– Every good and perfect gift is from above, coming down from the Father of the heavenly lights, who does not change like shifting shadows. God is an unchanging, consistent Father. Human fathers are often unpredictable. 2 Timothy 2:13 – If we are faithless, he remains faithful, for he cannot disown himself. Never doubt God's love for you another day of your life, He cares for you all the time no matter the weather, He is unchanging.

Mother Teresa says Spread love everywhere you go; first of all, in your house. Give love to your children, to your wife or husband, to a next-door neighbour. Let no one ever come to you without leaving better and happier. The biggest disease today is not leprosy or cancer or tuberculosis, but rather the feeling or being unwanted, uncared for, deserted by everybody. The greatest evil is the lack of love and charity, the terrible indifference towards one's neighbour who lives at the roadside, the victim of exploitation, corruption, poverty, and disease.

Darkness cannot drive out darkness: only light can do that. Hate cannot drive out hate: only love can do that. Learn to light a candle in the darkest moments of someone's life.

Be the light that helps others see; it is what gives life its deepest significance; we are to become an agent of change in peoples' lives by pulling people out of darkness into His marvellous light. We move specific people from the darkness of sin to the light of Christ. Reach out to people, get to know people, be the salt of the world, be the light of the world. Engage in what we called surface-level interaction and conversation with your neighbours — not just to be polite, but to love the people by getting to know them. Show interest in their welfare knowing the fact that you cannot influence people at a distance. Get into the habit of asking good questions to generate meaningful conversations. Learn the art of drawing people out. Dialogue at deeper levels displays the beginning of a more meaningful friendship. This takes time, good listening, thoughtful questions, and being vulnerable and open. Explore friendship with your neighbour and you will experience the same.

Best Friend –The Big Daddy Above

What a friend we have in JESUS! He is interested in our affairs; so, lets Him have free access to all aspects of our lives. **Joel chapter three verse fourteen - Multitudes, multitudes in the valley of decision: for the day of the Lord is near in the valley of decision.**

Life is made up of an infinite number of choices. Most decisions, such as what you'll eat for lunch today, are small and only slightly impactful, but it's the big decisions—the ones that can change your life forever—that are tough to make.

We are the creative force of our life, and through our own decisions rather than our conditions, if we carefully learn to do certain things, we can accomplish those goals. Your life changes the moment you make a new, congruent, and committed decision. Life presents you with so many decisions. A lot of times, they're right in front of your face and they're really difficult, but we must make them. There are different types of decision processes. Common types of decision-making processes.

Majority decision-making process. Hierarchical decision-making. Proportional decision-making. Consensus Decision-Making but individual decision-making processes are in four categories: analytic style, conceptual style, directive style, and behavioural style. If you have arrived at your decision with the sincere intention of pleasing the heart of God, incorporating biblical principles and wise counsel, you can proceed with confidence knowing that God will work out His purposes through your decision. God doesn't want people to do what they think is best: He wants them to do what He knows is best, and no amount of reasoning and intellectualizing will discover that.

Ruth 1:15-16 Then she said, "Behold, your sister-in-law has gone back to her people and her gods; return after your sister-in-law." But Ruth said, "Do not urge me to leave you or turn back from following you; for where you go, I will go, and where you lodge, I will lodge. Your people shall be my people, and your God, my God. Choices are the hinges of destiny. Decisions made can be excellent, good, fair or bad completely. I believe that we are solely responsible for our choices, and we have to accept the consequences of every deed, word, and thought throughout our lifetime. It might seem good to make decisions too fast because you don't want to be seen to be dragging your feet but you must understand that haste could make waste; making decisions not well thought through can be damaging, so take your time. Urgency and despair don't get along well. Ruth decision to follow her mother in law had positive impact on her life and the future generations.

Nothing happens until you decide. Make a decision and watch your life move forward. You are the CEO of your own life, start making executive decisions today. It is in your moments of decision that your destiny is shaped. An ignorant man follows public opinion. Every decision brings with it some good, some bad, some lessons, and some luck. The only thing that's for sure is that indecision steals many years from many people who wind up wishing they'd just had the courage to leap. Always go with the choice that scares you the most, because that's the one that is going to help you grow.

There are people who make decisions just to keep other people happy and yet we come to discover that right decisions are seldom the popular decision. Saul made a decision that destroyed his destiny.

Don't base your decisions on the advice of those who don't have to deal with the results. You are only one decision from a totally different life. In the end, we only regret the chances we didn't take and the decisions we waited to make. You cannot make progress without making decisions. Life is filled with difficult decisions, and winners are those who make them. Decisions should not be made in fear. Fear paralysis. Fear is destructive.

Fear immobilises hence decisions made based on fear might be destructive to our destinies or our callings. We are to walk by faith and not by fear.

Aristotle Said, it is easy to fly into a passion--anybody can do that-- but to be angry with the right person to the right extent and at the right time with the right object and in the right way--that is not easy, and it is not everyone who can do it.

You experience life changes the moment you make a new, congruent, and committed decision. Oftentimes, the most important decisions are the most difficult to make - for, your future, and the future of the generations that come after you, hinges on the outcome of those decisions.

Life is about choices. Some we regret and some we are proud of. Some will haunt us forever but remember there is always balm in Gilead. The message: we are what we chose to be. Decisions shape our destiny. The wrong decisions can lead you down the wrong path, whereas the right decisions can lead you down the right path.

Learn from your bad decisions and improve upon them, as your daily decisions determine the life that you will live. Unsuccessful people make decisions based on their current situation; successful people make decisions based on where they want to be. A real decision is measured by the fact that you've taken a new action. If there's no action, you haven't truly decided. When decisions are made while angry it can be detrimental to your progress in life. Emotional based decisions can be very destructive hence be careful.

Deal with your emotions in a correct manner. Always remember that anger is one letter short of danger. Whatever the situation is - no matter how aggravated and angry you feel, staying cool and keeping your mind calm always pays off for the better. Anger and laughter are mutually exclusive and you have the power to choose either.

You don't have to accept the invitation to get angry. Instead, practice forgiveness, empathy and encouragement. The Big Daddy is never mad at us despite our shortcomings! **Robert K. Greenleaf, The Servant as Leader says On an important decision one rarely has 100% of the information needed for a good decision no matter how much one spends or how long one waits. And, if one waits too long, he has a different problem and has to start all over. This is the terrible dilemma of the hesitant decision maker.**

It is imperative to emphasise that we are solely responsible for our choices, and we have to accept the consequences of every deed, word, and thought throughout our lifetime. It might seem good to make decisions too fast because you don't want to be seen to be dragging your feet but you must understand that haste could make waste; making decisions not well thought through can be damaging, so take your time.

Urgency and despair don't get along well. Choices are the hinges of destiny. Decisions made can be excellent, good, fair or bad completely. Decisions are the frequent fabric of our daily design.Decisions can be made too slowly.

Please understand there are times when a fast decision is easy; even prudent provided you know the right answer and if it has a biblical basis. Your decisions as a child of God should be God centred and God focused. Waiting hurts. Forgetting hurts. But not knowing which decision to take can sometimes be the most painful. You never know when your life is about to change. You never know when one decision will dramatically impact your life and change the course of your destiny nonetheless you still have to make decisions in life; believers' lives are made easier when making decisions because of the help that is made available to us through the Holy Spirit. There are times when delaying a decision has benefit. Often, allowing a set period of time to mull something over so your brain can work it through generates a thoughtful and effective decision. If you have a decision to make, list down the pain points of doing it and the pleasures of doing it too.

Jillian Michaels was of the opinion that Whenever you're making an important decision you should, first ask if it gets you closer to your goals or farther away. If the answer is closer, pull the trigger. If it's farther away, make a different choice. Conscious choice making is a critical step in making your dreams a reality. Do not look down on others and never assume the position of monopoly of wisdom. Proactive decision-making process is great but ultimately making reactionary decision could have a negative impact on you.

At some point in their lives, each one of us requires mentoring, guidance and counsel to get better clarity on our vision, passions, goals, and life in general. Dr Prem Jagyasi. It takes a level of self-love, of dedication and determination to live your greatest life. So, look within. Look at every area of your life and ask yourself these questions: Am I on course? Am I growing mentally, emotionally and spiritually? Anything that is blocking that, anything that is preventing you from living your greatest life, make the tough decision to let it go.

TAKE NOTE #11

—

Dominion

In the jungle:

- The Elephant is the biggest
- The Giraffe is the tallest
- Fox is the wisest
- The Cheetah is the fastest

Yet, the Lion is the KING of the jungle even without ANY of the qualities outlined above. Why? Because:

- The Lion is courageous, is bold, walks with confidence, dares anything and is never afraid.
- The Lion believes it is unstoppable.
- The Lion is a risk taker.
- The Lion believes any animal is food for him.

- The Lion believes any opportunity is worth giving a trial and never lets it slip from its hands. So, in life:
- You don't have to be the fastest.
- You don't have to be the wisest.
- You don't have to be the smartest.
- You don't have to be the most brilliant.
- But you have to be courageous
- You must have the will to try.
- Believe it is possible.
- Don't doubt God's ability in you to do the supernatural with God on your side you can move mountains.

Ironically, the Lion sleeps for 20 hours but works for only 4 hours and amazingly still eats meat. But the elephant works for 24 hours but eats grass only; your days of eating grass are over. Your life's strategy matters most in your approach to circumstances and situations in winning the race of life. Stay in the Lion's mood! That's the mood for winners! Always stay in your lane, fulfilling your calling and mandate. Life exam questions are never the same hence answers to life questions are bound to differ; if there are two of you, one of you is unnecessary.

CHAPTER 13

New Day

It is a new day for a new thought, new identity, new ideas, new steps and new breath! We may choose to repeat the mistakes of yesterday or think of the lessons from the mistakes of yesterday. We may choose to dwell on the fortunes or misfortunes of yesterday or think of what we can do with the fortunes or misfortunes of yesterday today! We may choose to continue or discontinue the steps we took yesterday today. Life is here today and we must think of what we can do today for today was the vision of yesterday and the true foundation of tomorrow! Ernest Agyemang Yeboah

The past can leave us in an indelible bitterness. The past can erode our present joy. The past can chain our present in the cage of the past. The past can make our future look blurry but we have a choice to learn the lessons of the past errors and start on a clean slate. You will rise above all limitations once you begin to live life with the right attitude. **People who fail and fall are the people who see difficulties in every opportunity and call it "impossibility". Rise up!** IsraelmoreAyivor.

Nothing good stands without the right attitude. You may know how to do it, but if the attitude is negative, all you can say is "I could have done it." Stop going to work to earn just your hourly wage. Successful people are always looking for ways to get to the next step up to the next level in life. Instead of showing up to work to earn your hourly wage, show up as if you were learning how to run the place. Develop a positive attitude to make a difference in the world of duplicates.

Be thirsty for new challenges, be hungry for growth by giving your best at your current position and work place, invest your life to enrich others and always be willing to learn by taking on new responsibilities. The obstacles that stood in the way of our next level must be cleared out; we are people of God and the best has been reserved for us.

Living in the present moment, we feel encouraged and motivated in our lives; we sit on solid ground and are not easily knocked off our balance into discouragement and negativity. James Adler. Do not focus on the challenges at hand; stop focusing on the clouds and see the silver lining. When you are focusing on the mistakes, the errors, errata and setbacks that you are going to have to deal with and not seeing them as an opportunity to learn, you are only hurting yourself. Successful people learn to analyse their mistakes and accept them as lessons.

Mistakes have the power to turn you into something better than you were before. Anonymous. We all make mistakes; have struggles and even regret things in our past but you are not your mistakes so don't allow those mistakes to stop you from fulfilling your purpose in life.

Never make excuses. Your friends don't need them and your foes won't believe them. John Wooden. Making excuses will rob you of your potentials. Excuses will cast shadow on your integrity hence stop those excuses TODAY. Your complaints, your drama, your victim mentality, your whining, your blaming, and all of your excuses have NEVER gotten you even a single step closer to your goals or dreams. Let go of your nonsense. Let go of the delusion that you DESERVE better and go EARN it! Today is a new day! Steve Maraboli.

When it rains, it pours. But soon, the sun shines again. Be confident. Better days are on their way. Do not despair. Do not quit. Do not fold your arms. Do not allow procrastination to rob you of your destiny, do what you have to do NOW as God does not promise us TOMORROW. Have faith in tomorrow, for it can bring better days. Never wish for yesterday, for it has gone its separate ways. Believe in today, for it's what you're living now. Tonya K. Grant. If you were a quitter, you would have given up on life a long time ago. The fact that you're still here proves that you're a fighter with hopes of better days. Sonya Parker We cannot afford to walk through life without understanding our reason for existence, for without purpose, life has no meaning. Where there is no purpose for living, fulfilment becomes evasive.

As a matter of fact, the need for a higher purpose is so paramount to the human soul, that the Bible says, where there is no vision, the people perish." It is a dangerous thing to be alive without understanding why you were given life. The very second you begin to doubt is the minute you lose sight of your outcome. Even in our darkest hour, will we find better days. Don't let the years pass, reflecting the light that becomes your shadow. Richard Tovish.

Finish each day and be done with it. You have done what you could; some blunders and absurdities no doubt crept in; forget them as soon as you can. Tomorrow is a new day; you shall begin it well and serenely and with too high a spirit to be encumbered with your old nonsense. Ralph Waldo Emerson.

Prayer 4 Today

I PROPHECY THAT GOD WILL CONTINUE TO OPEN
DOORS OF OPPORTUNITY FOR YOU; DEBTS WIPED
CLEAN, BILLS PAID IN FULL - HENCEFORTH GOD
WILL EMPOWER YOU TO DO THE IMPOSSIBLE.I
SEE GOD SCATTERING EVERY DREAM KILLER
AROUND YOUR DESTINY; YOUR LEVEL OF RESULTS
WILL DISAPPOINT YOUR ADVERSARIES.I DECREE
PLEASANT SURPRISES IN EVERY AREAS OF YOUR
LIFE. I DECLARE THIS DAY THAT HELP HAS COME
YOUR WAY HENCEFORTH. THIS IS YOUR SEASON
OF RESTORATION, RECOVERY, PEACE AND
COMFORT.THAT CHALLENGE YOU ARE FACED
WITH COMES TO AN END TODAY. AS FROM TODAY
YOU WILL WALK INTO HIGH LEVEL OF FAVOURS,
YOU WILL CONTINUE TO PROGRESS IN LIFE IN
JESUS MIGHTY NAME.

HENCEFORTH, YOUR JOY SHALL BE FULL AND
YOUR TESTIMONY SHALL BE PROFOUND. AS
FROM TODAY, YOU ARE BREAKING THROUGH
ALL SPIRITUAL GATES AND LIMITATIONS TO

POSSESS YOUR POSSESSION. YOU ARE SUPREMELY BLESSED AND HIGHLY FAVOURED. THE CLOTHES THAT COVER YOUR NAKEDNESS WILL NOT TEAR. YOUR PAST WILL NOT HOLD YOUR FUTURE TO RANSOME. THE PILLARS THAT YOU REST UPON WILL NOT FALL. HENCEFORTH RECEIVE THE POWER AND SPIRIT OF FOCUS AND DETERMINATION TO BECOME WHAT YOU ARE WIRED TO BECOME.

THE VERDICT OF DEATH AND HELL OVER YOUR LIFE AND THAT OF YOUR FAMILY ARE HEREBY REVOKED. YOUR FAITH SHALL NOT BE DEFLATED. YOUR HOPE SHALL NOT BE SHATTERED. YOUR TOMORROW SHALL NOT BE IN DISARRY. YOUR PEACE AND COMFORT SHALL NOT BE THREATENED. YOUR JOY SHALL NOT BE STOLEN. WHAT YOU HAVE LABOURED FOR WILL NOT BE BLOWN AWAY BY THE STORMS AND WINDS OF LIFE. PROBLEMS AND TRIALS OF LIFE WILL NOT TAKE AWAY YOUR SONGS OF PRAISE NOR REMOVE LAUGHTER FROM YOUR MOUTH.

CHAPTER 14

Ditch Worry

First Peter chapter five verse seven says: Give all your worries and cares to God, for He cares about you. Instead of worrying about what you cannot control, shift your energy to what you can create. Worry does not empty tomorrow of its sorrow; it empties today of its strength. We challenge you to use your energy creatively thereby adding value to your life. Don't waste your time in anger, regrets, worries, and grudges.

Life is too short to be anxious. It's going to take more than your willpower to stop worrying. You need God to step into your situation. No amount of regretting can change the past, and no amount of worrying can change the future. Never let the future disturb you. You will meet it, if you have to, with the same weapons of reason which today arm you against the present. The more you pray, the less you'll panic. The more you worship, the less you worry. You'll feel more patient and less pressured. Worry pretends to be necessary but serves no useful purpose. The greatest tragedy of life is not unanswered prayer, buy unoffered prayer. Do not be timid to pray because it is your given right as a child of God. The story of every great Christian achievement is the history of answered prayer; may you receive answers to your prayers.

Fear imprisons, faith liberates; fear paralyzes, faith empowers; fear disheartens, faith encourages; fear sickens, faith heals; fear makes useless, faith makes serviceable. God is able to do more than you ever imagine! Keep trusting God. Your miracle will surely come through. How would your life be different if…You should stop worrying about things you can't control and started focusing on the things you can. Let today be the day you free yourself from fruitless worry, seize the day and take effective action on things you can change. Pray, hope, and don't worry. Worry is useless. God is merciful and will hear your prayer. To be worry free you have to live one day at a time. The only courage that matters is the kind that gets you from one moment to the next. Happiness is achieved when you stop waiting for your life to begin and start making the most of the moment you are in. We can't rewind the past, nor fast forward the future, so today, all we can do is play, record, pause and keep moving …

Worry is most often a prideful way of thinking that you have more control over life and its circumstances than you actually do. We tend to be preoccupied by our problems when we have a heightened sense of vulnerability and a diminished sense of power. Today, see each problem as an invitation to prayer. You have to trust God to care. You can only pray if you trust God enough to take care of your needs.

Worry is itself an illness, since worry is an accusation against Divine

Wisdom, a criticism of Divine Mercy. Drag your thoughts away from your troubles... by the ears, by the heels, or any other way you can manage it. Worry is a misuse of the imagination. Never worry alone. When anxiety grabs your mind, it is self-perpetuating.

Worrisome thoughts reproduce faster than rabbits, so one of the most powerful ways to stop the spiral of worry is simply to disclose your worry to a friend, in person of JESUS. The simple act of reassurance from the Lord [becomes] a tool of the Spirit to cast out fear -- because peace and fear are both contagious. **STOP TRYING TO WORK THINGS OUT before their times have come. Accept the limitations of living one day at a time. When something comes to your attention, ask Me whether or not it is part of today's agenda. If it isn't, release it into My care and go on about today's duties. When you follow this practice, there will be a beautiful simplicity about your life: a time for everything, and everything in its time. — Sarah Young**

TAKE NOTE #12

—

How to sleep: The healthy habit to avoid before bed - could harm your heart warns expert

The cumulative effects of sleep loss have been linked with a host of deleterious health outcomes. Drinking most of your water mid-morning or mid-afternoon may be preferable to avoid heart trouble, experts have warned.

Drinking water throughout the day is important to avoid dehydration - but it can hinder health if done late at night. The common habit often leads to frequent bathroom trips throughout the night. By interrupting the <u>sleep</u> cycle, the body may suffer long-term hormone fluctuations that could put the <u>heart</u> in danger.It is a well-known fact that the body needs seven to eight hours per night for optimal health. This is because sleep helps the body control hormones which are implicated in stress and metabolism.

If sleep disturbances become chronic, the body is likely to experience frequent fluctuations in hormones. These hormonal disturbances are responsible for high blood pressure, and other metabolic complications such as type 2 diabetes and obesity. All-cause mortality is also increased in men with sleep disturbances. According to the Centers for Disease Control and Prevention, these problems are frequent in people who sleep less than seven hours per night.Unfortunately, the average person in the UK gets roughly six hours of sleep per night, due to various factors such as frequent trips to the bathroom.

Aqua Pura's hydration expert, Doctor Stuart Galloway, of the University of Stirling, said: "When it comes to evening hydration, it is recommended to drink between 300 and 500 ml of liquids two to three hours before going to bed. By Express Health ..

CHAPTER 15

No Place for Envy

When everything goes great in our lives, we might still be unable to find peace, especially since great success means a greater chance to arouse feelings of envy and jealousy that ruin our relationships. Envy is a heart problem. Any time you envy you have gotten your worship misguided, because envy is a form of worship. Sometimes, success and envy are two sides of the same coin. Jealousy is the fear of comparison. Jealousy is usually the result of a comparison that puts us in a negative light.

We are jealous because we either recognize our shortcomings and become bitter because of them or because we are insecure and fail to acknowledge our own greatness. The problem that envious or jealous people fail to recognize is the ones tormented by their feelings are actually themselves. Their feelings torment them excruciatingly, while the objects of their envy or jealousy can easily ignore their attitude and move on with their lives. Envy blinds men and makes it impossible for them to think clearly. Envy doesn't only make us angry and bitter, but it also clouds our judgment, making it impossible to choose correctly what is best for us. Envy wastes your time and energy.

Envy has the power to distort our views and to impede us from thinking rationally. Jealousy is a weird feeling. It stems from love and it is able to cross all the way to hate. Combining love and hate, jealousy is never a feeling that we should hold on to because it is unhealthy and eventually ends up destroying the love. When envy flourishes unity and oneness of purpose is destroyed. We are only as strong as we are united, as weak as we are divided. We are each other's harvest; we are each other's business; we are each other's magnitude and bond. When spiders unite, they can tie down a lion. So powerful is the light of unity that it can illuminate the whole earth. Unity and victory are synonymous.

> *There is a magnificent, beautiful, wonderful painting in front of you! It is intricate, detailed, a painstaking labour of devotion and love! The colours are like no other, they swim and leap, they trickle and embellish! And yet you choose to fixate your eyes on the small fly which has landed on it! Why do you do such a thing?*
> — *C. JoyBell C*

Envy denies your uniqueness. Envy blinds you to your own giftedness and uniqueness. But God didn't make you to be like somebody else. God made you to be you. Envy, after all, comes from wanting something that isn't yours. But grief comes from losing something you've already had. **Greed, envy, sloth, pride and gluttony: these are not vices anymore. No, these are marketing tools. Lust is our way of life. Envy is just a nudge towards another sale. Even in our relationships we consume each other, each of us looking for what we can get out of the other. Our appetites are often satisfied at the expense of those around us. In a dog-eat-dog world we lose part of our humanity."** — **Jon Foreman.** Listen,

If the grass is greener on the other side of the fence, you can bet the water bill is higher. — *Debbie Macomber,*

Blessed is he who has learned to admire but not envy, to follow but not imitate, to praise but not flatter, and to lead but not manipulate. — William Arthur Ward. Envy makes us critical, intolerant and judgemental which are never good lens to see people through. We exaggerate the minor flaws of those we envy so we can feel greater than them. On the other hand, love does the opposite, by minimizing the flaws as they wouldn't even exist. You are uniquely and wonderfully made hence there is no reason to envy your brother or sister. The worst thing about envy is that no matter how smart, kind, generous, beautiful or accomplished we are, there is always someone even better than us, which means that if we are not careful, we can never escape the grip of envy.

We rise by lifting others. Be nice to people... maybe it'll be unappreciated, unreciprocated, or ignored, but spread the love anyway. We rise by lifting others. Happiness has two hands: one with strength for lifting up heavy hearts and a gentle hand for tickling. You become strong by lifting others up, not pulling them down. No one is useless in this world that lightens the burdens of another. There is no exercise better for the heart than reaching down and lifting people up. Accept the past as the past and realize that each new day you are a new person who doesn't need to carry old baggage into the new day with you. It's amazing how many people ruin the beauty of today with the sorrows of yesterday. Yesterday doesn't exist anymore. Think about every good thing in your life right now. Free yourself of worrying. Let go of the anxiety, breathe. Stay positive, all is well. Your story will end in PRAISE. You are next in line for a major BREAKTHROUGH. Great people do not look down on others nor push people down and this is also one of the attributes of happy people. What will you benefit by dragging others in the mud? It is your responsibility to treat others well. Every time you mistreat someone, you reveal the part of you that lacks love and needs to heal. See the light in others, and treat them as if that is all you see.

Spread love not hate. Negativity is NOT normal. Believing in negative thoughts is the single greatest obstruction to success. Beware of those who are bored and not passionate about life, for they will bore you with reasons for not living. Your thoughts carry you wherever you want to go. Weak thoughts don't have the energy to carry you far!

Envy occurs due essentially to comparison, stop comparison today!Comparison is an act of violence committed against one's self. Clyde Lee Dennis. Every flower bloom at a different pace. Excel at doing what your passion is and only focus on perfecting it. Eventually people will see what you are great at doing, and if you are truly great, success will come chasing after you. When we accept the labels placed on us by ourselves and others, we then restrict and limit ourselves based on those labels. Break free from them and reclaim your unlimited potential to be your amazing self.

Comparison is the most poisonous element in the human heart because it destroys ingenuity and it robs peace and joy. Euginia Herlihy. You are UNIQUE so do not compare yourself with others; if there are two of you one of you is unnecessary. Do yourself a favour never compare yourself to others because comparison swallows your God given gift. Comparison is bad news, stay away from it as far as possible. Whatever your passion is, keep doing it. Don't waste time chasing after success or comparing yourself to others.

TAKE NOTE #13

—

Elon Musk

The richest person in the world at $190 billion as at 2022 is Elon Musk. Born, Elon Reeve Musk June 28, 1971 Pretoria, South Africa.Citizenship South Africa (1971–present), Canada (1971–present), United States (2002–present)

The Chronicle of Elon Musk

In 1995 he unsuccessfully applied for a job at Netscape.In 1996 he was ousted as CEO from a company he founded — Zip2. In 1999 the first product of PayPal was voted as one of the ten worst business ideas.In 2000 he was ousted from his company — PayPal — while on a honeymoon.In that same year, he almost died from cerebral malaria.In 2001 the Russians refused to sell him rockets he wanted to use to send mice or plants to

Mars.In 2002 the Russians turned him down again — This is what gave him the impetus to start SpaceX.In 2006 his first-ever rocket launch ended in an explosion and millions of dollars lost.In 2007 his second rocket launch ended in an explosion and millions of dollars wasted again.In 2008 his third and critical rocket lunch which also had NASA satellites onboard failed and exploded during lunch.In December of that same year, both Tesla and SpaceX were on the brink of bankruptcy. In 2013 his rocket failed during landing in the ocean.In 2014, the Tesla model had several problems with spontaneous battery combustion.In 2015, he had a second and third explosion while attempting to land his rocket on a drone ship.In that same year, he had a fourth rocket explosion at launch.In 2016, Tesla Model X deliveries were delayed for more than 18 months.In that same year, his rocket exploded at launch for the fifth time with Facebook's satellites for Africa onboard. The project was worth $300 million.

That same year, his rocket failed while attempting to land on a drone ship for the fourth, fifth, and sixth time.In 2017, he successfully launched a rocket into space and Tesla electric cars became the best-selling cars.After several failures, Elon Musk has now mastered the art of failing successfully.His net worth is

$167.2 Billion — as at December 2020.He is also, the Founder, CEO, Lead Designer of SpaceX.CEO, Product Architect of Tesla, Inc.Founder of The Boring Company and X.com (now PayPal)Co-founder of Neuralink, OpenAI, and Zip2Chairman of SolarCity. Elon Musk has showed why failing is important to achieve what we want.

Billionaires lose millions to become billionaires. Millionaires lose thousands to become millionaires. But the poor don't want to lose anything, so their fears make them prisoners of poverty.Failure is an option here. If things are not failing, you are not innovating enough —Elon Musk. When something is important enough, you do it even if the odds are not in your favour. —Elon Musk

Don't fear failure. Fear being in the exact same place next year as you are today. — Mel Robbins. Be Inspired.

ETIQUETTE

1. Don't call someone more than twice continuously. If they don't pick up your call, presume they have something important to attend to;

2. Return money that you have borrowed even before the other person remembers asking for it from you. It shoes your integrity and character. Same goes with umbrellas, pens and lunch boxes;

3. Never order the expensive dish on the menu when someone is giving you a lunch/dinner. If possible, ask them to order their choice of food for you;

4. Don't ask awkwatd questions like 'oh so you aren't married yet?' or 'don't you buy a car? for god's sake', it isn't your problem;

5. Always open the door for the person coming behind you. It doesn't matter if it is a quy or a girl, senior or junior. You don't grow small by treating someone well in public;

6. If you take a taxi with a friend and he/she pays now, try paying next time;

7. Respect different shades of opinions. Remember what's

6 to you will appear 9 to someone facing you. Besides, second opinion is good for an alternative;

8. Never interrupt people talking. Allow them to pour it out, as they say, hear them all and filter them all;

9. If you tease someone, and they don't seem to enjoy it, stop it and never do it again. It encourages one to do more and it shows how appreciative you're;

10. Say "thank you" when someone is helping you.

11. Praise publicly. Criticize privately;

12. There's almost never a reason to comment on someone's weight. Just say, "you look fantastic." If they want to talk about losing weight, they will;

13. When someone shows you a photo on their phone, don't swipe left or right. You never know what's next;

14. If colleagues tell you they have a doctor's appointment, don't ask what it's for, just say "i hope you're okay." Don't put them in the uncomfortable position of having to tell you their personal illness. if they want you to know, they'll do so without your inquisitiveness;

15. Treat the cleaner with the same respect as the ceo. Nobody is impressed at how rude you can treat someone

below you, but people will notice if you treat them with respect;

16. If a person is speaking directly to you, starting at your phone is rude;

17. Never give advice until you're asked;

18. When meeting someone after a long time, unless they want to talk about it, don't ask them their age and salary;

19. Mind your business unless anything involves you directly - just stay out of it;

20. Never talk about your riches in the midst of the poor. Similarly, don't talk about your children in the midst of the barren... or talk about your spouses around those who don't have.

Unknown Author

CHAPTER 16

Sustaining Hope

May your life overflow with hope through the power of the Holy Spirit. God is the source of life. Life without God is hopeless. But life with God is an endless hope. No one can foretell the details in a day, we can only hope. I do not know the details of tomorrow, but I have a hope for a better tomorrow. Hope is the confidence of brighter tomorrows. Lailah Gifty Akita. Faith is very optimistic that all is well. By Faith, the elders obtained a good report; if they obtained a good report under the old covenant, it means you can obtain an excellent report under this dispensation of GRACE; the new covenant.

To think to win is to stay alive. Take ownership of your thought life. Fight for what is yours; defend your territories. Take possession of your inheritance, right NOW. No matter how bad you feel, God never sees you as a reckless person. He may see you as a sinner who needs to be re-washed to get back to his old vision for His purpose, but He will never see you as a hopeless being who was created for nothing. Now if God will not see you as hopeless, why then should you see yourself that way? Be bold to say am qualified to dominate the world. It is awesome to be able to stand tall and say – I fell apart, and I survived. If you fail, never give up because F.A.I.L means – FIRST ATTEMPT IN LEARNING. End is not the end. In fact, E.N.D means – EFFORT NEVER DIES.

If you get NO as an answer, remember N.O means – NEXT OPPORTUNITY. If you feel like you are losing everything, remember that trees lose their leaves every year and they still stand tall and wait for better days to come. Life is not always easy. Unfortunately, things happen to us and we don't know why. Life can sometimes leave us feeling down in the dumps. We shut down and think the pain we feel is never going to end. Pain is inevitable. Suffering is optional. Micah says: Do not rejoice over me, my enemy; when I fall, I will arise; when I sit in darkness, the Lord will be a light to me. When you are knocked down by the issues of life, do not despair because God has got your back. Things might be bad for a while but if you do not quit, it is guaranteed that a new season will come your way. Your dignity can be mocked, abused, compromised, toyed with, lowered and even badmouthed, but it can never be taken from you. You have the power today to reset your boundaries, restore your image, start afresh with renewed values and rebuild what has happened to you in the past.

Faith is always about NOW while HOPE is always about the future. If a man loses hope he will commit suicide, to lack hope is to give up completely. Hope is a great necessity for producing and sustaining the enthusiasm required to live a purposeful and fulfilling life. You have to see beyond the mountains confronting you, you must see God in the midst of the trauma. See the victory. Life's trials will test you, and shape you, but don't let them change who you are. Those who achieve the extraordinary are usually the most ordinary people because they have nothing to prove to anybody. Although no one can go back and make a brand new start, anyone can start from now and make a brand new ending.

You are wired to win battles. You are wired to be an overcomer. Your faith will be tested and challenged. You must hang in there, not quitting. Those who lack hope quit pursuing their dreams. You cannot afford to turn your back on your MANDATE. If you remain hopeful you will be able to go the distance in life. God will fight your battles if you just keep still. He is able to carry you through. Trust Him. Keep standing, keep believing and keep hoping. Don't be discouraged by life's difficulties. With hope and determination, you can triumph over any difficulties.

Until you see victory it will not happen. **Success in life is not for those who run fast, but for those who keep running and always on the move. — Bangambiki Habyarimana.** Quitting produces regrets later in life; so, you are admonished never to quit. Don't lose hope because hope enables you to stay in the game until a solution is found. Sustaining your hope can help you keep on until a solution is found.

Perseverance is failing 19 times and succeeding the 20th. Don't let the fear of losing be greater than the excitement of winning. When the word says - Hope in God: scripturally speaking means, to use the words of William Carey, "Expect great things from God. Working hard for something we don't care about is called stressed; working hard for something we love is called passion. I love the way the psalmist wrestle, fight and struggle to maintain his hope in God. Without hope, you have no power to absorb the wrong and walk in love, and you will sink into self-pity or self-justification. Hope in God, hang in there. Biblical hope is not a mere desire for something good to happen. It is a confident expectation and desire for something good in the future. Biblical hope has moral certainty in it.

> *Progress is like wheels that never stop; they have to keep turning in order to remain relevant to a car and all of its mechanical parts. Stopping is not an option in real time but it is to those that envy progress and upward mobility. Progress never ends because it is infinite but it rebuilds and readjusts (s) to take increment steps then massive steps if it is hindered.*
> Terrance Robinson.

Helen Keller said, Keep your face to the sunshine and you cannot see a shadow. With God, you are stronger than your struggles and fiercer than your fears. God provides comfort and strength to those who trust in Him. Be encouraged, keep standing, and know that everything's going to be alright.

Count your smiles instead of your tears; Count your courage instead of your fears. Unknown. Many of the things you can count don't count. Many of the things you can't count really count. Albert Einstein. Do what you needed to do today, don't delay again, it's time for action. Procrastination is like a credit card; it's a lot of fun until you get the bill – Christopher Parker. Procrastination is not a sin but it is a weight! Avoiding your responsibilities is not a sin but it's a weight. T.D Jakes. Times and conditions change so rapidly that we must keep our aim constantly focused on the future. There is nothing permanent except change. Just take any step, whether small or large. And then another and repeat day after day. It may take months, maybe years, but the path to success will become clear.

Most people have no idea that tragedy and silence often have the exact same address. When your day is a museum of disappointments, hanging from events that were outside of your control, when you feel like your guardian angel put in his two weeks' notice two months ago and just decided not to tell you, when it seems like God is just a babysitter that's always on the phone, when you get punched in the oesophagus by a fistful of life. Remember, every year two million people die of dehydration. So, it doesn't matter if the glass is half full or half empty. There's water in the cup. Drink it and stop complaining. Muscle is created by lifting things that are designed to weigh us down. When your shoulders are heavy, stand up straight and call it exercise. Life is a gym membership with a really complicated cancellation policy. Remember, you will survive, things could be worse, and we are never given anything we can't handle. When the whole world crumbles, you have to build a new one out of all the pieces that are still here. Remember, you are still here. The human heart beats approximately 4,000 times per hour and each pulse, each throb, each palpitation is a trophy, engraved with the words " You are still alive." You are still alive. So act like it." — *Rudy Francisco.*

The Hallmark of a Conquerors

- Making God number 1 by walking in FAITH and not by SIGHT as Faith has the capacity to turn dreams into realities and promises to possession. They are clear about God's purpose and plan for the assignment at hand.

- Know of a certain that victory has already been obtained with the evidence of celebrations and shouting of Hallelujah

- Credit all warfare and operational successes to God, alone.

- Willingness to speak to the mountains

- They are not ignorant of when REST is needed

- Not lose sight of REWARD as in the case of David verses Goliath

- They are not lazy, static nor lay about but rather they keep pushing against all oppositions, taking territories thereby making a mark.

- Know and Understand the secret of preservation - it is more difficult to preserve than to conquer; preservation require an investment.

TAKE NOTE #14

---

8 Ways Cabbage is good for everyone

- **Fights inflammation**
- **Keeps you strong**
- **Improves digestion**
- **Protects your heart**
- **Lowers your blood pressure**
- **Lowers cholesterol**
- **Maintains bone health and healthy blood clotting**
- **Keeps cancer at bay**

8 Health Benefits of Cabbage – Cleveland Clinic

CHAPTER 17

Fearlessness

You are mandated to be fearless. You are expected to be bold as a lion ..Every bird of prey looks over its shoulder before it goes in for the kill, even a hawk. Even they know to watch their backs – every single one but an eagle. It's fearless. Michelle Horst, Wake Me Up. God uses your pain to help others. This is called redemptive pain; it is the highest and best use of the pain you go through. God does not want you to waste a hurt. Our pains are useful, they are precious; the experiences can be transformative and become a great blessing to others.

Our stories hold unique inspiration for one another. Lailah Gifty Akita. In life, pain is inevitable. Whether physical or mental, we all deal with pain on a daily basis. No pain, no palm; no thorns, no throne; no gall, no glory; no cross, no crown. William Penn.

There is no bandage to stop the tears, no method to sterilize the psychic wound, and no plaster cast for the heartbreak. What we do have is our presence, and by listening to the needs of the suffering, we provide a connection that is more powerful than any spoken words of wisdom. Sandra Hamilton.

Some people hate you because you know that you are an eagle and they want you to think you are a chicken so that you will peck at the ground looking for ants and worms, so that you will never know that you are an eagle and always think yourself a chicken.

Let them hate you, they will always be chickens, and you will always be an eagle. You must fly. You must soar." Said the old owl. C. JoyBell C.

The eagle has no fear of adversity. We need to be like the eagle and have a fearless spirit of a conqueror. Joyce Meyer

Many times, it happens we live our life in chains and we never even know we have the key. The Eagles. I hate the survival word. It just shows that you are adjusting your life in hope of living. Life must be like an eagle. Full of self-respect, proudly, independently, painfully, kind, valuable. Otherwise, cockroaches also living on this Earth and easily killed for hygiene. What is the use of that survival? SonalTakalkar. You will never see an eagle of distinction flying low with pigeons of mediocrity. Onyi Anyado.

The Bible often uses the symbol of an eagle to portray strength, power, vision, and even destruction. The Biblical analogies using eagles should inspire us to righteous living and strengthen our walk with God.If an eagle is teaching you to fly, ignore the advice of turkeys. An eagle never loses sleep over a turkey's sentiments. MatshonaDhliwayo. Eagles: When they walk, they stumble.

They are not what one would call graceful. They were not designed to walk. They fly. And when they fly, oh, how they fly, so free, so graceful. They see from the sky what we never see. Anonymous. Why fly like a hen when you can soar like an eagle? Pio of Pietrelcina. When everything seems to be going against you, remember that the airplane takes off against the wind, not with it. Henry Ford. Take up an idea, devote yourself to it, struggle on in patience, and the sun will rise for you. Swami Vivekananda. f you haven't started, then taking action is more important than finding the best strategy. If you're already taking action, then ensuring you're working on the right thing is more important than working harder. Your effort sets your floor. Your strategy sets your ceiling. James Clear.

TAKE NOTE #15

—

Demotivation

Reasons why you feel demotivated

- Unfruitful relationships
- Though an Eagle but Keeping company with fowls
- Pursuing meaningless goals
- Limiting beliefs or Self-doubt
- Civil war – fighting yourself, turning the sword on yourself
- Not playing to your strengths
- Stuck in a rut or Roundabout experience
- Excuses - He who excuses himself accuses himself. You can either make excuses or make progress

CHAPTER 18

God's Factor

God has work for you to do because you are relevant in His equation. You matter to God. You are not a waste of space. You are not a statistic. God has a specific assignment for you. Right from the beginning God created you in such a way that you could fulfil the divine purpose for which you were created. He ordained, or planned, the works to fit you and you to fit the works. Let your door stand open to receive Him, unlock your soul to Him, offer Him a welcome in your mind, and then you will see the riches of simplicity, the treasures of peace, the joy of grace. Throw wide the gate of your heart, stand before the sun of the everlasting light.

The book of Mathew chapter six verse thirty-three says -But seek ye first the kingdom of God, and his righteousness; and all these things shall be added unto you. To fall in love with God is the greatest romance; to seek him the greatest adventure; to find him, the greatest human achievement. God is creating in you the right desires and then He is giving you His ability to do what he wants you to do. You will never understand who you are until you understand who God is!

Spending time with God is the key to our strength and success in all areas of life. Be sure that you never try to work God into your schedule, but always work your schedule around Him. Joyce Meyer

Jesus taught that your highest priority must be your relationship with Him. If anything detracts you from that relationship, that activity is not from God. God will not ask you to do something that hinders your relationship with Christ.Stubborn, rebellious, stiff-necked people miss the great things God has for them because they refuse to let God work in them. He is working on those who let Him because He will never force Himself on people. God is not a gate crasher. Remember: He WANTS your fellowship, and He has done everything possible to make it a reality. He has forgiven your sins, at the cost of His own dear Son. He has given you His Word, and the priceless privilege of prayer and worship.

God has never responded to potential. He never works in your life relative to your need of Him. He responds to passion. He is not overly impressed by what He gives you. He responds to your reaction to the gift. What you do with the gifts He stored in you decides the favour of God. Happiness comes from clarity. It comes from deciding who we are, what we value, and how we will spend our lives. And that comes from taking time to think clearly, make smart choices, and plan wisely. The universe is wired with the electricity of God, and each of us is a lamp. It doesn't matter the size or shape of the lamp; it only matters that the lamp is plugged in. With every prayer, every thought of forgiveness, every meditation, every act of love, we plug in.

The more of us who plug in, the more the darkness of the world will be cast from our midst. Today, let's all increase love's wattage! Embrace His love for you for He cares passionately for you. Dying for me was the most He could do but living for Him is the least I can do. The problem is that instead of turning to God and letting Him fill our souls, we turn to other things — pleasure, fame, money, sex, or drugs and alcohol. Some people even turn to false philosophies or religions, hoping these will lead them to the truth and fill the empty place in their lives.

I will live for God. If no one else does, I still will. When you finally realise this world cannot help you, you will cry out to the one who can. We must be ready to pursue God relentlessly. Pursuing and yearning for God is how we grow spiritually. Of course, our desire for God doesn't start with us — it starts with God's desire for us! "

I have come to see clearly that life is more than self. It is more than doing what I want, striving for what will benefit me, dreaming of all I can be. Life is all about my relationship with God. There is no higher calling, no loftier dream, and no greater goal than to live, breathe, and be poured out for Jesus Christ. What a friend we have in Jesus ....

A life without Jesus Christ is a life devoid of total fulfilment. When you have Jesus then you have peace and hope for the future; a life filled with light. Life without Jesus Christ is like two things: a) a journey without a destination, b) a pencil which has no point.A life with Christ means a life of peace, security, fulfilment, joy, direction and the absence of fear.The empty places in our hearts were created to be filled by God alone; if God set you free – stay free, I admonish you not to return to what made you miserable, which in my opinion was sin. Hang around Jesus so that your sins can be washed away. Jesus alone can take care of our ugliness.

For a seed to achieve its greatest expression, it must come completely undone. The shell cracks, its insides come out and everything changes. To someone who doesn't understand growth, it would look like complete destruction. Life does not accommodate you; it shatters you. Every seed destroys its container, or else there would be no fruition. — Cynthia Occelli

==============================

When your trust has been betrayed, the only thing to do is live, learn and let go. Otherwise, the betrayal done by another will turn into hate for them. But they will not feel this hate; it will only hurt you more, growing bigger and darker. So, live, learn and let go. By living, it means they did not hurt you so deep that you cannot move forward. Learn; learn to not trust this person again, and to make more of a sound judgement in the future. Letting go doesn't mean forgetting. It means that you have let go of the pain it caused. And by not forgetting, you will learn and move forward from the betrayal of the past. — S.L. Vaden

When we let go and stop dragging the pain of the past, we free ourselves of dead weight and allow our hearts to heft the good stuff...the stuff that makes our journey lighter, easier, and more meaningful. — Toni Sorenson

==================================

Your complaints, your drama, your victim mentality, your whining, your blaming, and all of your excuses have NEVER gotten you even a single step closer to your goals or dreams. Let go of your nonsense. Let go of the delusion that you DESERVE better and go EARN it! Today is a new day! — Steve Maraboli

Stop Glorifying the Devil!

Reflection - STOP MAKING THE DEVIL FAMOUS

"The Devil is a liar" shouted his wife as she tried to turn on the car.

"How is the Devil a liar? What has the Devil done this time?" He asked his wife as he sat on the passenger seat. She was to drive today.

"Well, we've run out fuel and we need to get to the Church event quickly. I am preaching today and the Devil is trying to frustrate me.

The Devil is a liar" she said then declared some Bible verses.

He laughed and looked to the side.

"What are you laughing at?" She asked him turning to face him.

"Why are you making the Devil famous?" He asked her.

She looked at him surprised. Giving him that shhhpiritual face.

"Honey, the Devil is not to blame for the low fuel, we are. You forgot to go to the petrol station yesterday after the visit from your mom. You are giving the Devil too much credit.

When things go wrong it is not always the Devil's fault. He is not that powerful. Many times it is just a matter of poor human decisions and laziness" he said.

She looked at him intently.

Silence.

He smiled and continued, "Yes honey, like the day we were financially struggling. That wasn't the Devil plotting against us. It was just us who were making a mess and not making good financial decisions. We were borrowing too much, spending too much and living above our means.

Once we got more disciplined, we attracted wealth. Look at us now, we were able to buy a new car and we've built our own home"

She unbuckled her seat belt and listened to her husband.

"When we were struggling to raise our teenage daughter. It wasn't the Devil who was messing our family. It was us as parents who didn't take time to understand how to raise a teenager. We didn't listen to her, we were talking down at her demanding respect and believing that since we love God she will tow the line. Once we went for the parent's seminar and we learnt the strategy on how to raise a teenager, our relationship with our daughter has improved. She even tells us she loves us these days, she hugs you, takes us out for lunch occasionally" he continued.

She sighed.

"When I applied for that job that I wanted so much. We prayed and prayed about it. But the truth is, I didn't get the job, not because of the Devil as we used to say; but because I wasn't qualified.

The most qualified person got the job. I wasn't blessed by it, but God blessed another with it. And look how things turned out. Because I didn't get the job, I ventured into business and look at how successful I have been" he told her.

She put out a smile.

"When our marriage was going through difficulty and we used to say that the Devil has cursed us, we used to wonder whether we were carrying generational curses since both our parent's marriages failed.

We were wrong. The moment we put effort to better our communication and to spend more quality time together, our marriage improved" he said looking at her smile.

"When we had a car accident. That wasn't the Devil as we used to say! That was my fault, my recklessness for driving while exhausted, battling fatigue.

It was a bad choice, not the Devil.

Many Christians are used to blaming the Devil thereby shifting responsibility from themselves.

They don't work on their mess and much of what they do is say the Devil is at work.

Many marriages are failing, not because the Devil is this powerful being succeeding; but because of laziness, irresponsibility and indecision by the couple.

So no Honey, we will not make the Devil famous. We will declare more about God's goodness and be good stewards of our blessings.

We will not live in fear thinking the Devil is coming for us yet we have God on our side to protect us.

We will take responsibility. When we fail to do something, we will own up and do better" he spoke further.

"Have I ever told you how much I admire you my amazing husband?" she told him.

He smiled and said, "You can tell me one more time"

She kissed him and said, "I love you. Honey, let's board a taxi.

We don't have much time.

The sermon I am going to preach has changed. I will preach on exactly what I have learnt from you:

Stop making the Devil famous.

No more giving the Enemy that has been defeated free publicity" Anonymous

CHAPTER 19

The Fighters

It is often said that peace is not simply the absence of conflict or any other artificial state the world has to offer. Rather it is the deep, abiding peace that we can find only in Christ Jesus. — *Billy Graham*

Dreaming was easier than screaming, and screaming was easier than worrying, and worrying was easier than crying, which was what she knew she would be reduced to if she didn't keep a hard eye on herself. — *Kevin Brockmeier*

Don't be lazy. Don't be passive. Don't fold your arms. Don't put up I don't care attitude. God cannot steer a parked car! Don't tell God you're waiting on him. Do something. Turn on the ignition, and just start driving. Get going. Be proactive. Where? Anywhere! Get involved in building destinies. Get involved in Kingdom matters. Ditch Excuses; be hungry for RESULTS; desire upward movement. Ditch MEDIOCRITY; ditch procrastination; ditch compromises; divorce grasshopper mentality, walk away from chickens because you are an eagle; keep company with your mates.

If you do not take charge of your life, who will do it for you? We have a mandate to do what is right and doing so would mean exercising greater self – control and fight for what belong to you. Do not allow your emotions overrun your life, take back control. You have power over your mind - not outside events; self-control is one of the fruits of the Spirit and yes, you can be in control. The best fighter is never angry. Anger is one letter short of DANGER. Never respond to an angry person with a fiery comeback, even if he deserves it...Don't allow his anger to become your anger. Self-control is the chief element in self-respect, and self-respect is the chief element in courage.

You must major on the major and never major on the minor. Some people tend to be more solution-oriented, and others more problem-oriented.

There is always a solution to any challenging situation. Being a Christian does not mean that we suspend our five senses, they are gifts from God to humanity and they must be used effectively to better our lives. Identify your problems but give your power and energy to solutions. Whatever the problem, be part of the solution. Don't just sit around raising questions and pointing out obstacles. Every problem has a solution. You just have to be creative enough to find it. **If the**

challenge exists, so must the solution. Rona Mlnarik. It might be a challenge for some of us to take charge of our lives. Prominent among the reasons why that might be the case is getting glued to the past. Please understand that the past is dead, buried and cannot be cured. There is nothing you can do but to bury the past.

> *When you are intense, you will do things persistently and with speed. The ability to be intense in whatever you do is a key factor in reclaiming your lost years. The totality of your commitment will make you more efficient. You need to understand the principle of intensity to reclaim time. You need speed to regain your lost years. You have to be pragmatic, purposeful and goal-oriented to be fully effective.* — Sunday Adelaja

When God has you in a waiting period, don't put your life on hold. Instead, imitate the habits that grow strong faith. Get spiritually busy knowing fully well that spiritual warfare is not a video game. Talk to the Big Daddy above for He will cover your head in the day of battle. The function of prayer is not to influence God, but rather to change the nature of the one who prays. Let us never forget to pray. God lives. He is near. He is real. He is not only aware of us but cares for us. He is our Father. He is accessible to all who will seek Him. God shapes the world by prayer. **The more praying there is in the world the better the world will be, the mightier the forces against evil. — E.M. Bounds.** Fight on your knees; bend your knees and conquer. Prayerlessness is a declaration of independence from God. It is STUPIDITY and ARROGANCE to refuse to pray. **The more you pray, the less you'll panic. The more you worship, the less you worry. You'll feel more patient and less pressured. — Rick Warren**

> *We tend to use prayer as a last resort, but God wants it to be our first line of defence. We pray when there's nothing else, we can do, but God wants us to pray before we do anything at all. Most of us would prefer, however, to spend our time doing something that will get immediate results. We don't want to wait for God to resolve matters in His good time because His idea of 'good time' is seldom in sync with ours. — Oswald Chambers.*

TAKE NOTE #16

—

Ways To Suppress Your Weight Gain Hormones

- **Aim for a High-Fibre, Low-Sugar Diet:** Insulin is one of the hormones which has been linked to weight gain, since it encourages cells to take the sugar you eat and store it in your body as fat. This begins a vicious cycle: as you put on weight, your body requires more insulin to bring sugar into the cells, which in turn encourages you to put on weight.

- **Choose Your Dairy Wisely:** Unless you are lactose intolerant or have a specific allergy to milk, dairy products as such aren't bad for you. But you need to choose those products wisely. Many large dairy owners in the industry have been using <u>artificial growth hormones</u> in their cows for years to stimulate the production of milk and meat and while this may increase profits, the hormones in this milk – which were not designed for humans – has been linked to weight gain and the early onset of puberty for those who use them regularly.

- **Eat Protein Throughout the Day:** While you don't have to pile on the steaks and pork chops with every single meal, it is a good idea to eat a little protein throughout the day. This doesn't always have to be animal-based foods like meat, eggs, or dairy but can also include nuts and seeds and legumes (beans, lentils or peas). Why is the protein so important? It has been shown that a diet with adequate amounts of protein helps to regulate a hormone called <u>Ghrelin</u>.

- **Skip the Soy Products:** Soy is tricky: while it is a low-fat, low-calorie, plant-based source of protein, it also contains chemicals called phytoestrogens that can block the utilization of real estrogen in the body.

- **Be Careful of Grains:** Grains – especially whole grains – aren't necessarily bad for everyone. However, if you have a problem with sluggish thyroid hormones, you might want to seriously cut down on them. Several studies have found that a grain-rich diet can have the effect of slowing down the thyroid even further. This is a problem, since thyroid hormones are some of the most important players in the weight loss game: they help to regular the metabolism,

- **Reduce Caffeine intake:** Coffee and tea are not as demonized as they used to be, since researchers have found that these drinks are also rich in antioxidants that can provide the body with a wide array of health benefits. However, if you are trying to lose weight, you might want to consider seriously watching your caffeine intake. Why? Caffeine can raise the levels of cortisol, the now-infamous hormone that rises in response to stress and signals to your body that it is time to pack on the fat, especially in the abdominal area, where it does the most harm - Brian Wu

Other Books by the Author

Freedom From Mediocrity

The Pyramid

Strategic Positioning

Other books: Co-Authored

Refreshing - Steve Adewole and Honour Adewole

The Link – Steve Adewole and Honour Adewole

Revolution - SteveAdewole and Honour Adewole

Contact details, below:

WWW.WHORG.ORG

Email: info@whorg.org

Tel: 02085973990

Mobile: 07883687099

Purchase your copy from Amazon

Printed by Amazon Italia Logistica S.r.l.
Torrazza Piemonte (TO), Italy

42040649R00100